Copyright © 2023 Partners for Education, Agriculture, and Sustainability. All rights reserved.

No part of this publication may be reproduced, stored in, or introduced in to a retrieval system or transmitted, in any form or by any means (electronic, mechanical, photocopying, recording, or otherwise), without the prior permission of the publisher. Requests for permission should be directed to training@peascommunity.org. Individuals may only physically reproduce supplementary lesson materials for students so long as programming is free to students.

CREDITS

Artwork in "Nature's Palette" Lesson provided by Juliet Whitsett

Graphic Designer: Callie Gabbert

Copy Editor: Kate Rowe

PEAS (Partners for Education, Agriculture and Sustainability) is a 501c3 nonprofit organization based in Austin, TX. Founded with the mission to cultivate joyful connections with the natural world through outdoor learning and edible education. PEAS delivers unique, outdoor learning and edible education programs to participating school campuses, operates and maintains a community farm, runs camps, leads professional development and provide consultation to help teachers and schools bridge key science, nutrition, math and health concepts from the garden to the classroom. Delivering programming year-round, PEAS provides trained outdoor and edible education specialists who partner directly with classroom teachers at each school's campus to lead outdoor and kitchen lessons, increasing students' time spent learning in an outdoor, hands-on environment.

Learn more at peascommunity.org

First Edition: Printed in the U.S.A.

Table of Contents

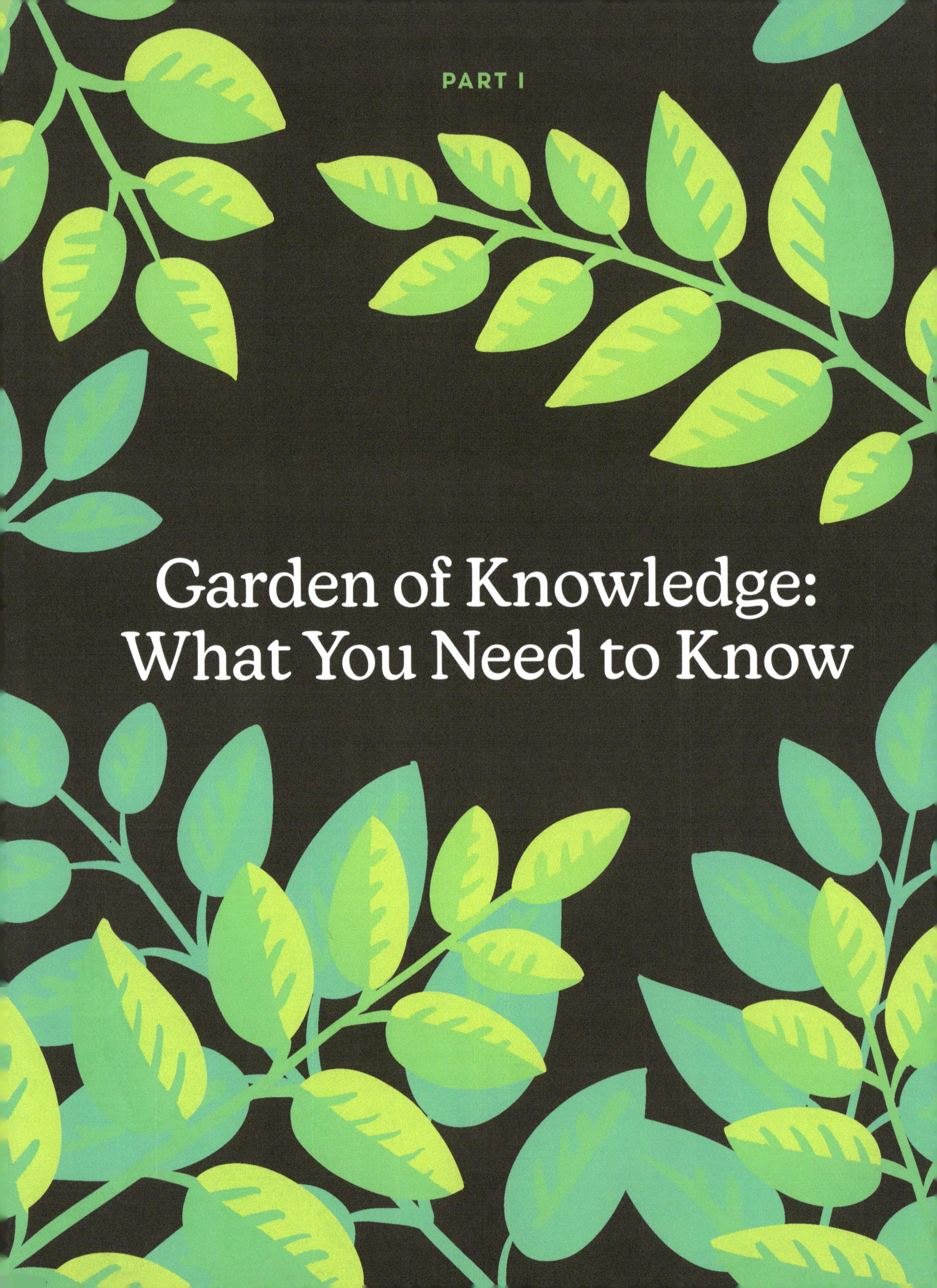

Garden of Knowledge: What You Need to Know

This book is for teachers, by teachers.

Are you new to teaching outdoors?

Are you groovin' along the path, but looking for ideas and inspiration?

Maybe you want to fine-tune your advanced practice?

Looking to enrich a homeschool program with backyard and garden exploration?

Well, this is the guidebook for all of you!

All authors and major contributors to this guidebook are staff at PEAS — Partners for Education, Agriculture, and Sustainability — in Austin, Texas. PEAS' mission is to cultivate joyful connections with the natural world through outdoor learning and edible education. PEAS is a passionate community committed to carving out time and space for students to connect with the Earth we all share. PEAS began its year-round, school day program in the fall of 2016, and we have learned so much along the way.

© 2023 Partners for Education, Agriculture, and Sustainability

As an organization, we are devoted to connecting with nature, with the understanding that we humans are of the natural world ourselves. PEAS is striving to dismantle the idea of the human and nature binary that exists in much of our society. We will be referring to our *outdoor* lessons in reference to their location, since we *are* nature at all times. Lessons in this guidebook are designed to be place-based in any educational setting no matter the extent, or lack, of green and/or outdoor learning features. Expansive gardens on the edge of a forest aren't necessary for students to experience the wonder and awe of the organisms on our planet. Our team takes our lessons to local schools across our city in an effort for students to participate in exploring the natural world wherever they are.

As former classroom teachers who now focus all of our time leading students outdoors, we have created this guidebook that is easily accessible to educators with tight schedules and offers a mix of pedagogy and practice. While these lessons have been designed with second and third graders in mind, you will find they are easy to adapt for younger and older students or homeschool settings. You will be surprised by the connections and academic risks your youngest students will take, and delighted by the joy and enthusiasm your "too cool for school'' fifth graders will exhibit.

Part I walks you through the why and how to prepare both mentally and physically for taking lessons outside for learning.

Part II focuses on the social and emotional aspects of learning outside and how being outside can nourish the whole child.

Part III provides lessons across disciplines that are easy to implement and build on for future lessons. These lessons are designed to take place on school grounds or in community green spaces.

Part IV is for those who want more. This section leads the reader to an abundance of resources where they can learn more about outdoor education, find a plethora of curricula and lessons, and learn about other organizations that are supportive of this work.

We hope you find this guide to be Easy PEASy and user friendly!

Lauren Zappone Maples is the founder and Executive Director of PEAS — Partners for Education, Agriculture, and Sustainability. PEAS began grassroots as a Community Farm and Urban Orchard on the campus of Cunningham Elementary in 2011. In 2015 Lauren became the founding executive director of PEAS, the nonprofit, in order to provide outreach outdoor and edible education programs to Austin-area schools. Prior to leading PEAS, Lauren was a classroom teacher with Austin Independent School District, worked as environmental educator for the City of Austin, and taught as an adjunct professor at two local universities. She has received multiple awards for her work centered around place-based outdoor and edible education, including the John F. Ahrns Award for Environmental Education from the Westcave Discovery Center in 2014 and 2021, the Fulbright Distinguished Award in Teaching Grant in 2015 and a Fulbright Alumni Grant in 2017, and the SlowFood USA Snailblazer Award for school garden education in 2021. Her research has been highly influential in the development of programs, community initiatives, and the long-range organizational goals of PEAS.

Lauren has fond memories of exploring the urban creek beds of Austin as a child. She aspires to carve out time and space for herself and others to experience the wonder and awe she feels when she is outdoors.

© 2023 Partners for Education, Agriculture, and Sustainability

Mathew Garland is an award-winning teacher with over 20 years of experience in elementary education. As a public school teacher, he developed his campus garden, created a curriculum for bringing learning outside, and piloted a sustainable classroom model. Working with other district leaders, he helped to establish Austin ISD's Garden-to-Cafe program, which allows student-grown produce to be served in school cafeterias. He has led outdoor education professional development at the district level and is the recipient of various educational awards including Teacher of the Year. He founded Nearby Naturalists, a children's nature club, and created a companion set of digital curricula to support outdoor learning. Mathew joined PEAS in 2022 and works as a Co-Manager of Curriculum and Training and as an Outdoor Education Specialist, helping to cultivate joyful connections with the natural world through outdoor learning and edible education.

Mathew spent much of his childhood exploring the drainage ditches and bayous of suburban Houston, Texas, on an endless search for turtles and snakes. His mother established a rule that any new reptiles be brought to the front door for her inspection before being allowed into the house. His childhood love of reptiles, bugs and trees led to his passion for education beyond the classroom door.

Erin Magrath is a teacher, student, and advocate of equitable and inclusive education. Erin began her journey in education working in a rural community in Argentina, where she was the ESL (English as a second language) teacher for an entire community. In turn, she learned many valuable lessons, along with the Spanish language, from her time there and later teaching positions and travels throughout Central and South America.

Erin moved to Austin, Texas, in 2010 to attend the University of Texas postbaccalaureate program for Bilingual Education. In her 8 years as a Two-Way Dual Language Teacher in Austin Independent School District, Erin had the honor and privilege to teach and learn from Spanish-dominant and English-dominant students and families, weaving culturally relevant, project-based and community-oriented learning experiences into the bilingual curriculum. In her time as a teacher, Erin led her campus as a Social Emotional Learning and Creative Learning Initiative coordinator, bringing her passion for authentic, equitable, and whole-child learning experiences to her school community. She worked as a bilingual district curriculum writer and developed professional development opportunities on a campus and district level. After many years in the teaching role, Erin decided to once more become a student, in order to gain further knowledge and experience to serve her community. In 2022 she graduated with honors from Texas State University with a Master's in Elementary Education.

Ever since she began walking to school as a first grader, rain or shine, Erin has been humbled, excited, and inspired by the outdoors. Whether spending an afternoon gardening, walking her three dogs in South Austin, or undertaking a multi-day backpacking trip, she feels a connection to outdoor elements and is so fortunate to be able to bring these experiences and feelings to learning communities through her work as Co-Manager of Curriculum and Training at PEAS.

© 2023 Partners for Education, Agriculture, and Sustainability

Lauren Reneé Salinas-Garcia is deeply devoted to celebrating the natural world, as she journeys her path to reconnect to her own Indigenous roots and practices. As a teacher and Outdoor Education Specialist at PEAS, her passion lies in mentorship, youth advocacy, and awakening wonder and community among her students. She has experience working in nursery schools, summer camps, and elementary and high schools. In 2015 she transitioned from an early childcare center into youth services with the Parks and Recreation Department in San Marcos, Texas. Over the next few years, her path led her to work as a Teacher's Assistant for Austin Independent School District. This experience invigorated her passion for Outdoor Education.

Growing up an only child, Lauren Reneé was fascinated by the teachings of nature–her companion. Her first memory is being stung on her face by a hive of bees at age four. This instilled within her a deep reverence toward other living beings and honoring their sacred space and innate wisdom. Today, she is often landed on by honeybees and thanks them for opportunities to teach her students that we can conquer fears and explore nature while respecting all life around us. She believes one thing that remains constant is the human necessity for deep connection with the natural world and the equanimity this provides. Her core mission is to provide children an equitable and expansive environment with opportunities to elevate, explore, discover, and create in harmony with nature and community.

What to Wear and Bring

Learning outdoors can be a rewarding and transformative educational experience, but success outdoors means showing up prepared. Nothing can be more disruptive than arriving unprepared for your learning environment—even for the most experienced outdoor educators. Consider the following items before heading to your outdoor learning area.

Clothing

Seasonal clothing can be tricky when dealing with a class full of students. Here are some simple questions you can ask yourself and your students before heading outside:

- Do I need more clothing or less?
- Am I wearing layers?
- Would a hat help?
- Are my feet protected?
- Do I need gloves or protection for my hands?

Being able to shed or add layers can be helpful in regulating body temperature outdoors. It is also important to have a plan for where all those layers should go when they are taken off. Having a designated area for clothing (but not in a pile to avoid the spread of lice) and water bottles will help greatly reduce the need to send kids back outside looking for their missing items.

Rain coats and umbrellas should also be considered if you plan to be outside in soggy weather. Depending on your comfort level, there can be a lot of interesting things to explore on a rainy day. As always, never explore outside if lightning Is present, and wait 30 minutes from the last sound of thunder before heading outside.

One nonnegotiable in terms of clothing should be close-toed shoes. Wearing shoes that can protect from stings, burs, nettles and sharp tools will minimize the risk of injury and keep feet comfortable while outdoors. Make sure your students are aware of this in advance. Wearing active shoes is a good idea at school for many reasons. It is important to inform your students' guardians of this in advance and set the expectation that children arrive ready to learn in an outdoor setting. Sharing your outdoor schedule and expectations with families ahead of time can help ensure everyone arrives prepared for learning outside.

It is also important to think about what clothing you are comfortable wearing outside. Depending on your own style and campus norms, it may be uncomfortable to go outside in what you typically would wear to school. If the school (or your personal) dress code is not suited for outdoor activities, you may have to get creative. Is there a "casual" or "jeans" day at your campus? You may want to plan your garden lessons for one of those less formal days. You also might consider reaching out to your campus leadership and asking for allowance or leeway in dressing appropriately for outdoor lessons.

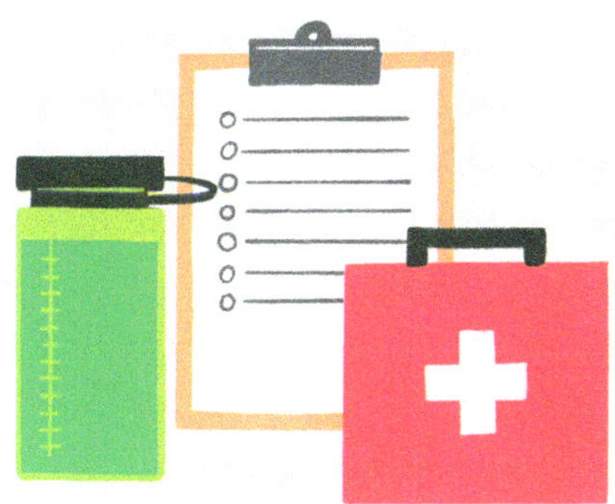

Must-Have Supplies

The supplies needed for outdoor learning will vary depending on the learning objectives for each outdoor lesson. However, there are some common supplies that you may want to consider having available for most outdoor explorations. When planning your outdoor lesson, it is important to consider the items that are always needed and those specific to the individual lesson. First, let's discuss the "must haves" for working with students outdoors.

WATER

Having ready access to water when outside will save valuable time and keep students hydrated and healthy. If your outdoor learning environment has an easily accessible water source, great! If not, it is important to have a plan for how children will quench their thirst, especially during hot weather days. While stopping for a water break on the way outside is always a good idea, it is important to have access to water outdoors. Students need hydration opportunities before, during, and after outdoor engagement.

Bringing water bottles to the outdoor area can be an easy accommodation if you plan ahead. Some things to consider include: How will the bottles be transported? Where will they be kept? How will you remember to bring them back with you?

Many teachers are already familiar with bringing water bottles to recess and may have a system such as a bin or wheeled cart to accommodate them. Visiting your outdoor area can utilize this same method. If you don't have a system, water bottles can simply be carried by students and stored somewhere shady near where you enter and exit from your learning area. This will help you remember to have students retrieve bottles when leaving and keep them from becoming scattered during your outdoor lesson.

Additionally, you may want water for your lessons and plants. Some exterior water spigots require a water key. Having one to access your school's faucet will be helpful. Water keys are inexpensive and can be found at your local hardware store.

FIRST AID KIT

Most injuries outdoors can be handled on-site by the educator or by campus nursing staff. Common non-emergency injuries while learning outdoors include small scrapes, splinters,

abrasions, minor skin irritation, bites/stings and eye irritation. Having a first aid kit with some key items can help manage these injuries and/or stabilize them while waiting for professional help. Common helpful items in effective first aid kits include:

- Antiseptic wipes
- Antibiotic ointment
- Antiseptic solution (hydrogen peroxide)
- Bandages and gauze
- Saline solution (to flush eyes)
- Disposable sterile gloves
- Epi-pen (if possible)
- Fine point tweezers
- Hydrocortisone cream
- Tissues

It is important to check your class files to see if any students have 504 Accommodations for pre-existing conditions and/or

allergies, and coordinate with the school nurse for individualized care. If a student experiences an injury or interaction that causes concern, always err on the side of caution and don't hesitate to call for emergency assistance.

Other Useful Items

TARP

If your outdoor learning area lacks seating, consider using a tarp for times when the class is seated together. Tarps are relatively inexpensive and allow for students to sit together even when the soil conditions may not be ideal. A tarp with a thickness of 10 millimeters or more will stand up to heavy use and can be used for many years. It will be helpful to have stakes or rocks on hand to anchor the tarp on windy days.

CLIPBOARDS, JOURNALS, & WRITING IMPLEMENTS

Writing surfaces can be hard to find outdoors, so make sure to plan for this in advance. If you wish to have students do any type of writing outside, a class set of clipboards or writing journals are very helpful. It is also a good idea to have a set of pre-sharpened pencils and a few hand sharpeners available.

BAGS OR BACKPACKS

If students have many personal lesson items to carry, it may be helpful to have them keep them in a specific outdoor learning bag or backpack that they can grab easily on the way out the door.

SUN PROTECTION & BUG SPRAY

Use of sunscreen and/or bug spray should be discussed with your students' adults in advance and be prepared to share what type of sunscreen you will be using and how it will be applied. Often families will have their own preferences about the use of these items and may want to send products from home.

It may be helpful to have a few umbrellas on hand for students who are extremely sensitive to the sun or don't quite fit under the shade structure.

HAND SANITIZER

Hand sanitizer can be a great short-term complement to handwashing. When in the garden, students should always have clean hands if they are going to taste any produce. Washing hands before leaving the classroom is ideal, but having hand sanitizer can help ensure hands are clean before handling produce.

FIVE-GALLON BUCKET AND PLASTIC CUPS

A simple five-gallon bucket and a class set of plastic cups makes an easy watering station. Five-gallon buckets are relatively inexpensive and available at any hardware store. Hardware stores are often happy to donate items like this if you mention you are a teacher and it's for your class. Asking students and families to collect plastic to-go cups can quickly get you a set. You can avoid hose accidents and difficulty sharing by simply filling the bucket and letting the whole class hand water using cups. Remember to always model pouring "slow and low and don't throw!"

WHEELED CART

As you can see, the list of items to bring outside can grow quickly. A wheeled cart can make a huge difference when transporting items to your outdoor space. It is not a necessity and the lack of one should not dissuade you, but it can be a helpful luxury. If a wheeled cart is not in your budget, a few milk crates can help transport items well, and there is usually a student who would appreciate the responsibility of helping to carry them.

Bring What Works for You

Don't let not being fully equipped become a barrier. We can all make progress toward teaching outdoors. Bring what works for you and make adjustments as you learn. The outdoors is a magical learning environment, and we can make the best of it with a little preparation and flexibility.

Getting to Know Your Outdoor Learning Environment

Before bringing your students outside, it is important that you have an understanding of your outdoor learning environment. Outdoor learning spaces vary depending on your specific campus. Students will make meaning in outdoor spaces whether they take places in thriving gardens or on the sidewalk in the front of your school. Visiting this space in advance will help you achieve better outcomes and ensure a safe and fun experience for your students.

Important Considerations Include

- Are there any specific features in the space that require a procedure? (Is a key needed for water access? Do other classes use the space?)

- Are there physical boundaries or do you need to establish these areas through discussion?
  Example: "We stay on this side of the tool shed."

- Are there any areas that students will need to handle with care?

- Are there specific areas designated for other stakeholders (PTA, FHA)?

- Is the space accessible for all students' physical needs?

Once you've determined the boundaries and protocols of your space, consider the following about your learning area:

Safety Plan

Whenever leaving the classroom, it is always important to have a safety plan regarding what to do in the event of an emergency. Make sure you know your campus procedures for all emergency situations, including where to bring your students, and make sure that you can return to the indoor environment with ease in the event of a lockdown or severe weather situation. It is also a good idea to include your outdoor learning times on a shared schedule, so that your class can easily be located by administration if the need arises.

Fire Ants and Other Wildlife

Check your learning area for potential organisms that need to be given space. Keep an eye out for fire ants (their mounds will be more pronounced above ground after rain). Mark insect mounds with small flags, traffic cones, or hoops to help students avoid them. Check under leaves and on branches for wasp nests, and be on the lookout for other potentially harmful organisms. Do not attempt to remove an active wasp nest, but know where it is located and share that location with your students. Alert your campus administration or maintenance

if a nest is in a high-traffic area, so they can make plans for its professional removal. Make note of any debris and stacked objects that could harbor small mammals, venomous spiders, and snakes. Locating these areas can help you determine what boundaries you will set for your students.

It's important to remind students that some organisms need space. While most organisms found outside are harmless, others may bite or sting. Establishing expectations for respecting nature is an important prerequisite to outdoor learning. Encourage your students to observe wildlife only with their eyes. We will discuss these procedures in more detail in our Top Ten Tips and Setting Expectations and Guidelines for Fun and Safety sections.

Remember that it is exciting to see wildlife! Practice beforehand with your students what to do during a wildlife encounter. The following steps will help your students have positive and safe interactions outdoors:

- Remain calm and quiet.

- Give space.

- Observe with eyes and ears.

- Share what you've found.

Having a plan in advance will help students feel confident

while observing and proud when they make a discovery. If a sting or bite occurs, remain calm. Remember to use your first aid kit and always consult with campus health professionals if there is an injury of concern.

Hazardous Objects

Looking for hazardous objects such as broken glass should be an ongoing concern. After an initial cleanup of these items, continue to monitor for any hazardous objects that could pose a threat. Teach students to report hazardous objects to you and never to handle them personally.

Water

Whether you are planning a vegetable or habitat garden, or just wanting to teach outside, a nearby water source is a great advantage. Planting a vegetable garden or wildlife habitat without an outdoor water source is a major hurdle. You may want to reconsider your location and find an area with accessible water if you are serious about starting a garden. If a water source is simply not an option, you can make the most of naturally occurring rainwater by some of the following methods:

- Install rainwater collection systems like cisterns and barrels.
- Manage the land using berms and swales or design a waffle garden to maximize captured rainfall.
- Install ollas in your garden to slowly release rainwater harvested using the collection systems mentioned above.

Rain

Eventually your outdoor plans will be affected by rain. Is there a covered area that will allow you to stay dry outside? If not, is there a place where you can observe the outdoors from inside? Remember that lightning is a nonnegotiable and you should head inside at the first sound of thunder.

Sun

Plan to visit your outdoor space during the time of day when you will be bringing your students. Make a note of where the sun is in the sky. It is important to know where the sun will be and how it might affect your students. Will the students be in full sun for the entire lesson? Does the sun create any obstacles to learning? Will the students need hats or sunscreen? Is there a shade structure or tree nearby that can mitigate the issue? Will changes of season create new challenges or opportunities? Consider the UV index before heading outside using a weather app, and make sure that students are not being exposed to harmful levels of ultraviolet radiation. If you plan to have the students sit for direct instruction, you will want to make sure that they are not facing into the sun. This rule of thumb will be discussed later, but if you have to choose between you and your students, the educator should always be facing the sun.

Shade

It is important to consider shade, both for relief from the sun, and also for any garden planting you may be considering. Does your space provide ample shade for hot days? Is there too much shade to plant a garden? Will lack of sunlight make the space too cold for students? Think about how trees, awnings, umbrellas, or shade sails might benefit or complicate your learning goals.

Sound

What do you hear when you visit our outdoor learning space? Are there any potential sounds that will make it difficult for students to hear a lesson? Is there a place nearby that might work better to introduce the lesson and reflect, while the exploration may still be okay taking place in the wildflower meadow next to the playground? Consider sound prior to your lesson to reduce frustrations for both you and your students.

Wind

It isn't always easy to prepare for wind, but having a few tips and tricks up your sleeve can help students focus. Prior to going outside, it may be useful to consult a weather app and set expectations for how to navigate issues that may arise in advance. A class set of clipboards to secure papers and provide a firm surface to write on is a key tool for outdoor education. Keep some rocks nearby to weigh things down if the wind picks up mid-lesson.

The More You Know

A firm understanding of your outdoor learning area before attempting your first lesson is imperative. That doesn't mean that you have to know and control everything about your space, but your outdoor learning experience will go much smoother with advance planning. Remember that outdoor learning requires flexibility. Be prepared to adjust due to conditions on a given day. The more you know about your space, the easier it will be to make adjustments on the fly.

© 2023 Partners for Education, Agriculture, and Sustainability

Setting Expectations and Guidelines for Fun and Safety

Outdoor learning is a valuable experience for students that sparks inspiration, new interests, and a different perspective on their world. The great potential of outdoor learning is most accessible when teachers establish clear expectations and safety guidelines. The criteria for outdoor learning can look, sound, and feel very different from classroom instruction, and teachers must prepare for this experience as much as students!

Teachers may introduce students to a natural space as a place of joy and learning, but also of respect, responsibility, and boundaries. Reminding students that we are nature, and looking at our surroundings with curiosity, empathy, and kindness can help them feel more connected to our planet. Student-led conversations that front-load how we carry ourselves outdoors, followed up by teacher modeling, can prevent negative experiences which lead to a fear or anxiety of the outdoors. They may also lessen concerns of students who have existing fears. Fun and safety expectations that we communicate to our students can shape their relationships to the natural world for a lifetime.

Front-load Student Expectations

All learners, young and old, are more invested and motivated to learn when given choice and agency. When students establish their own expectations for learning and safety before an activity through group conversations and decision making, they can better remember and follow their own guidelines. These conversations also provide explanations and important learning for students unused to outdoor spaces. "Why will we stay near the garden, and not go out to the field? Because when you are outside it is hard to hear when the teacher calls you." Students develop awareness of where they are and understand why there is a limitation.

When learning and interacting in an outdoor space, it is important to discuss with students beforehand how to respect and protect nature. Approaching potential encounters with plants and animals with empathy and connection creates a framework of stewardship for children at even the youngest ages. If you see a bug, do you squish it? Why or why not? In the outdoors, children learn they are in homes of plants and animals, and we must respect them, or as the saying goes, "treat them as we would like to be treated." Reflect upon the expectations you set in relation to your lesson. At times, you might want students to pick parts of plants. Explain that we always ask the teacher before we pick. Front-loading expectations in a student-led conversation will help them feel safer and more confident in their outdoor lesson. Because we spend most of our school day indoors, outdoor expectations are best reviewed before every lesson (and sometimes before each activity!) for students to be successful.

Below is a baseline of expectations for students and teachers during garden and outdoor lessons.

GARDEN EXPECTATIONS

Always walk in the garden and stay on pathways. Stepping in beds compacts the soil.

Respect each other, respect the wildlife, respect the plants.

Listen to learn. Listen to teachers and other students who are sharing.

Be safe with the tools.

Always ask before harvesting.

When you encounter a challenge in the garden, agree on a plan to overcome it.

Teacher Models Expectations and Safety

Students look to their teachers for cues for how to interact with nature. If a teacher runs and screams from a hovering bee, students are likely to do the same. Be prepared to model and demonstrate the emotional temperature you would like from your students. Model how to respect fire ants by leaving them alone, or how to remain calm with a nearby honeybee. If you would like students to interact with soil, plants or wildlife, model how to do so in a respectful and caring manner. We might tell students at one time to give insects space. If later we want them to collect bugs for an activity, we must ensure we model how to do so safely. Although some activities, like digging in the dirt or lying on the grass, might seem unneeding of demonstration, students can feel uncertain about even the simplest of outdoor actions. Students who watch teachers interact with nature with deliberate and calm movements are more likely to feel empowered to do the same.

Expect Learning to Look Different Outside

Spending time outdoors is proven to be a natural mood booster and energizer. That's probably one of the reasons you want to teach outside! Children are emotionally and physically stimulated outdoors. This creates wonderful opportunities for engagement, and in effect learning might look very different.

A strategy to help students be successful in their outdoor learning is the intentional practice of routines and procedures. To prevent pushing and crowding in an attempt to sit at once on a tarp, practice walking in a line and sitting down in one teacher-specified spot. Cut down on falls, garden damage, and accidents by taking a walking tour around the space. We recommend in the first (or first several) outdoor lessons to walk with students in a line and introduce areas of the garden or outdoor space, explaining the expectations for these areas. When students understand the implications, for example, of running in a garden bed so they don't compact the soil, or are explicitly told not to stand on benches for safety purposes, a teacher establishes clear boundaries which ultimately help students feel confident and safe in an outdoor environment. Understand that because outdoor lessons may not be in your daily routine, repetition of expectations or procedures may be important at the beginning of all outdoor lessons.

Furthermore, participation in your outdoor learning environment is great to model directly to students. Many teachers already have established routines for learning participation in the classroom, but it is helpful to repeat or modify these procedures outdoors. Practice student engagement techniques like turn and talk with students seated on the tarp. With the multitude of distractions and excitements, give students opportunities to model and apply listening skills and taking turns (by raising hands or any other routines you may use) in conversations with the class in this new space.

One of the most indispensable management skills in the PEAS approach is a defined and practiced "attention getter." In outdoor spaces, especially during activities where students might be spread out over a large area, it is useful to have a phrase that the educator calls out, to which students respond and know to give their undivided attention. Teachers have many examples of these in classroom settings. Know that even if an "attention getter" is an established routine, it might take students outside a couple of tries for full attention. At PEAS we enjoy changing our attention getter to the theme of our lesson as well. Other tools like a whistle, small instrument, or portable microphone call help students hear educators and give their focus with an "attention getter."

SOME GREAT OUTDOOR-RELATED ATTENTION GETTERS:

Teacher says, "Who-who?" like an owl, students say, "You, you," and make owl eyes with their hands as they look at their teacher.

Teacher picks an animal sound and says, "When you hear my rooster call, repeat the call back and look to me with voices off for your next set of instructions."

It is important to consider the many whirling thoughts, emotions, and connections exploding in a student's brain when they appear to be distracted or dysregulated. Read more about this in our section Letting Go for Learning.

To Know: Accidents Happen

Just like with any other situation on the playground or in the classroom, it is important to remain calm, as students are looking to you for how to react. Especially in the first few lessons outdoors, there is a higher chance of accidents as children test their limits and explore their surroundings. Know that regardless of how many conversations or details are within your safety and learning expectations, accidents can happen! Whether a bee sting, splinter or scrape, incidents during outdoor learning are a crucial reason to continue learning outside so students may reflect on past experiences. These are learning moments to help students make different choices and practice resilience. If an incident of concern occurs, you will want to follow your school's protocol and make sure guardians are in the loop.

© 2023 Partners for Education, Agriculture, and Sustainability

Garden and Outdoor Learning Jobs

Just as teachers establish jobs and task assignments in the classroom, this is a helpful expectation and management tool in the outdoor space. Outdoor jobs help students participate in their community and can also be a great support for you as a teacher. Depending on your learning environment, jobs for outdoor learning can be as simple as a student who helps sharpen their classmates' pencils or pulls a wagon, to more in-depth gardening skills and tasks. At PEAS, while our gardening tasks are implemented in different ways, we often have students rotate through the tasks so all have a chance to practice a variety of gardening skills. Alternatively, writing down a predetermined quantity of different jobs on popsicle sticks can give students choice over their work in the garden for that day. We encourage teachers to utilize jobs and roles in the outdoor classroom community to enhance a sense of community and responsibility for their outdoor space.

Reward Successful Lessons with Garden Free Time

When lessons go well, it's time to celebrate! Garden free time where students are allowed to discover, explore, or work in their desired way in the garden is a great reward and incentive for students. See our Resources section for a list of Outdoor Free-Time Choices if you would like to provide a list of options to your class.

Reflection After Outdoor Learning

Similar to best practices inside the classroom, closing a lesson with students reflecting upon their learning, but also their success in following expectations, is a metacognitive practice which helps students connect to the positive outcomes of following expectations and guidelines of outdoor learning. Take a moment after the lesson to have students discuss what they learned that day, what else they would like to know in connection to their learning, and then give feedback on how their compliance with expectations made them doubly successful. If students struggle to follow expectations, it is important to still find a positive quality to their learning before problem solving how they could improve for learning outdoors in the future. If any students had accidents that day, processing the cause and a solution to prevent future incidents with students is very important. Many students will see a hurt friend and be anxious they will be stung or hurt the next time they learn outside.

Paul Gorski recommends in the publication, Beyond Celebrating Diversity: 20 Things I Will Do to be an Equitable Educator to ask students what they liked and did not like about a lesson and to make changes from the students' feedback. This can be a very hard step to take as a teacher (who might have planned for hours to make an outdoor learning experience possible)! We encourage teachers to consider this practice as a part of their closing conversation and reflection process. If our goal is to have students feel participatory and connected to nature, they must feel the same agency in their educational journey. Know that it can take multiple experiences outdoors before teachers are able to get a read on the success of their lessons. Give your students and yourself grace with the amount you accomplished versus expectation. There is so much that students connect, explore, and learn when they interact with the outdoors that cannot be measured in a standard way, nor filled in on a multiple choice.

The experience of learning in nature for our student population is one of experimentation, joy, and discovery. Expectations and guidelines for outdoor learning are the foundation for a student's lifelong relationship with the planet.

Creating a Welcoming Outdoor Class

BY LAUREN ZAPPONE MAPLES,
FOUNDER AND EXECUTIVE DIRECTOR OF PEAS

Everyone wants to feel a sense of belonging. Everyone wants to feel loved. Unfortunately, it is impossible to ensure that every student feels that way every day when they walk through the doors of our schools. As educators, our focus of control is our classroom and the places we travel with our students, and it is our responsibility to do all we can to help our students feel like they belong and are cared for while they are with us.

In April of 2022, at the Growing School Gardens Summit in Denver, Colorado, I met with my colleague, district and school garden leader Neha Shah. We had the opportunity to sit down with a roomful of educators who spend time facilitating lessons with their students outdoors to discuss what a welcoming outdoor class feels like.

Below are some of the strategies we discussed that we agreed are the cornerstones for creating welcoming learning environments for our students. Knowing that each one of these could be expanded into a chapter of its own, it is our hope this will provide some food for thought and an opportunity to reflect on practice.

Create a culturally relevant learning environment.

- Get to know who you are sharing space with.
    - Knowing how they identify with regard to gender, culture, ethnicity, religion, language groups they belong to, and even politics is important and can influence how and what we teach.
    - Note your own biases. Be mindful of your internal monologue and any implicit biases you may bring to your teaching.
- Look for commonalities AND celebrate differences.
- Share stories of cultural wisdom, customs, and family practices related to content.
- Share stories that are meaningful and relevant to students' lives.
- When possible, invite diverse representatives from the community to share their experiences and stories.
- Install multilingual signage to represent cultures across the community.

Build an environment that encourages student voice.

- Choose activities that give all students an opportunity to share their thoughts and opinions. These do not have to all be within the same lesson but can be over time.
- Build a class culture that encourages students to feel comfortable sharing. Not all students will feel the same level of comfort when sharing with the group, and they will have preferences for when and how they want to share. With this in mind, here are a few ways to help build a classroom culture that helps students feel open to sharing:
- Give a variety of ways for students to share.
    - Vocally
    - Sticky notes
    - Mini chalkboards
    - Hand-raising
    - Holding up a particular number of fingers
- Set expectations for listening and speaking. Expectations will vary depending on whether activities are taking place with the whole class, small groups, or in pairs.
    - "When we are seated on the tarp, we use the same procedures we use indoors on the carpet."
    - "We use walking feet in our outdoor area so that everyone can feel safe."
    - "We keep tools below our waist to ensure we don't accidentally poke someone."
- Take note of who is sharing, who may want to share, and who is not comfortable sharing. Use this information to ensure all students who are wanting to speak up are able to.
- Consider using a talking piece such as a pine cone, feather, or small rock so all listeners know who they should be giving their attention to.

© 2023 Partners for Education, Agriculture, and Sustainability

- Encourage students to encourage each other: Using games can be a great way to encourage risk taking. The word bravo comes from the same root word as brave, which means to use courage or take a risk. Students rewarding each other with a "Bravo! Bravo!" is a fun and light-hearted way to encourage taking a risk.

- Provide opportunities for smaller group chats: Some students who may not want to speak in front of the whole class may be comfortable in a smaller group of their peers.
  - Think, pair, share
  - Shoulder partner chats
  - Table talk

- Circle up for sharing: When you want everyone to have the opportunity during the same lesson, choose a question or prompt a reflection that will give each student an opportunity to share. If time is limited, set parameters on how much each student should share (e.g. one sentence, three words, for 30 seconds, etc.)
  - Build sharing times into the routine.
  - Morning meetings
  - Opening and closing circles
  - Pre-lesson predictions, post-lesson reflections

Create a space for students to have choice about how they engage.

We all learn through multiple and different modalities and are drawn to engage with some activities over others. Creating lessons that allow students to have a say in what they do for at least a portion of the lesson can help a child feel like the lesson is relevant to their interests.

- Example: "Today we are going to visit three different activities, and then for the last 10 minutes of class, you will get to go back to the one you enjoyed the most."

Build in activities and roles within your lesson to help students grow their leadership skills:

- Station leaders
- Checklist readers
- Materials managers
- Record keepers
- Water filler
- Door/gate holder
- Waste manager

Know your students' unique needs and find ways to ensure content is accessible to them:

- English Language Learners
  - Visual aids
  - Use expression in speaking and with body language.
  - Repeat important instructions and information multiple times and in different ways.
  - Offer sentence stems for linguistic support to initiate conversations and stay on topic.
  - A variety of ways to discuss content and learning

- With hearing loss
  - Visual aids
  - Use expression in speaking and with body language.
  - Repeat important instructions and information multiple times and in different ways.

- Learning challenges
  - 504 Accommodations should always be provided in the outdoor learning environment.

- Behavioral challenges
  - Create a PEAce Area: an outdoor place where a student can take a break to regulate emotions.
  - Create special opportunities for students to take on responsibilities or tasks where they can be successful.
  - Provide two to three choices for participation (all choices are something you are okay with).

- Physically or mobility challenged
  - Consider how your outdoor learning area can be accessible to any student.

Understand your students' fears and create strategies with them to help them overcome them when possible. Not all fears need to be completely overcome. A healthy fear of stinging insects can protect us, but we don't want it to stop us from enjoying time outdoors. The goal is not to help students overcome all fears, but to help the individuals move along their own continuum to increase their comfort.

- Common fears:
  - Allergic reactions
  - Violence/trauma
  - Health issues
  - The unfamiliar/trying something new
  - Overstimulating environments
  - Being outside/open spaces
  - Insects/plants/dirt
  - Sun/rain/heat/cold
  - Tastes
  - Being wrong/not understanding
  - Peer judgment
  - Climate change
  - Work
  - Becoming a mermaid? Yes! Even some fears that may seem silly to us as adults can create barriers for our students. Accept that what may not make sense for us might feel very real to a child, and ask them for their ideas for what might help them cope with it.

- Strategies that may help:
  - Listen to and acknowledge student fears with compassion.
  - Provide a place and a space for students to express feelings about their fears.
  - Set goals with students.
  - Celebrate progress toward goals.
  - Discuss expectations in advance of going outside.
  - Be clear and specific about expectations.
  - Practice activities and routines.
  - Model behaviors, responses, and activities.
  - Repeat activities and routines so students know what to expect.
  - Repeat activities and routines so students know what to expect. (Did you see what we did there?)
  - Go slowly, and build on prior experience and knowledge.
  - Encourage progress, not perfection.
  - Be flexible and responsive to student needs.
  - Be playful when appropriate. Sometimes a little humor can go a long way when attempting to help a student recover emotionally.
  - Whenever possible, start young.
- Use open-ended questions to guide inquiry and promote exploration. Encourage curiosity, and create an understanding that there isn't always one right answer, and sometimes we may not find the answer at all.

© 2023 Partners for Education, Agriculture, and Sustainability

How to Support the Maintenance of Your Outdoor Learning Environment

One of the most important aspects of outdoor learning is the maintenance of your outdoor learning environment. Whether your space is a courtyard with potted plants, a simple circle of tree stumps in an open field, or a full-blown garden, it is important to enlist stakeholders who can help ensure your space is safe, inviting, and ready to provide for your students' needs. The initial push to get a garden started is not always the hardest part. Sustaining stakeholder interest from year to year can also be a challenge. Activating the space involves building a network of those with the desire to maintain the area. It can be slow, but over time can cultivate deep roots.

Campus Support

Outdoor learning is a proven benefit to education. Many administrators are now aware of the learning potential our outdoor areas can provide. If outdoor learning is new for your campus, consider letting the leadership know about your plans for taking learning outside. Dialogue with your administrator about partnerships that will support the outdoor learning environment. You may be surprised at their willingness to help. Your principal may be able to help in the following ways:

Custodial services: Informing your custodial team about your outdoor learning area can help to keep the area free of litter and maintained.

Campus funds: Some campuses have money set aside or are willing to write grants for learning initiatives. It's worth inquiring about what funds may be available for outdoor seating, raised beds, soil, tools, bird feeders, learning supplies (hand lenses and clipboards), or any other learning items you may desire.

Networks and partnerships: Administrators are often the recipients of communications from community partners willing to support the school in a variety of ways. Let the administrator know who the point of contact is leading outdoor education efforts.

District Support

Many school districts are also invested in the concept of outdoor learning. Check with your local district to see what resources may be available. Some districts have been known to provide the following:

- Grant money or grant writing
- Outdoor Learning Specialists
- Building supplies
- Curriculum
- Wellness committee
- Conference and professional development support
- Food service supplies

Homeschool Support

If you are a homeschool educator, there are many resources that you can access through your community. When we utilize our community partners, we model to students they are connected to a greater network. Here are a few of the many available resources that could facilitate your outdoor learning:

- Community gardens
- Local parks
- Nonprofit organization partners
- Libraries
- Recreational groups

Volunteers

Access to helpful volunteers can vary from school to school. Outdoor learning has a wide range of opportunities for volunteers to "dig" into, from weeding on weekends to assisting teachers as they lead lessons. If you have a local community that is eager to help, finding volunteers may be as easy as sending out an email. If your local community has difficulty finding time to volunteer, there are many other ways to find help:

Parents and family members: Many family members want to be involved with their children's schools but aren't sure how to plug in beyond being a member of the PTA/O. Communicating the time commitment and needs of the school or class is key.

Local businesses: Many businesses have service days where employees are encouraged to volunteer their time. Other companies offer grants that schools may seek to help with outdoor learning. Some companies have entire programs built around supporting school gardens.

High school helpers: Some high schools require their students to complete service hours. This can be an excellent way to find help and also can be a great bond between your students and their high school counterparts.

College interns: Many colleges require students in sustainability or nutrition programs to spend time volunteering in the community. Starting a relationship with a local college or university may create long-lasting support.

Others: Recreational and civic groups like Master Gardeners or Scouts

Nonprofit Organizations

Depending on your location, there may be nonprofits in your area that can support both program implementation and funding. See our Resources section for a list of national organizations, some with regional affiliations.

Local Businesses

Businesses often want to support their local schools and may be willing to make a financial sponsorship that can help fund outdoor learning activities and supplies. The business may want a sign or other recognition to show they are supporting the work. Make sure to factor any costs into the sponsorship proposal and that all stakeholders support the partnership.

© 2023 Partners for Education, Agriculture, and Sustainability

Many hands make light work!
If duties are divided into bite-size pieces,
they are more likely to get accomplished.

On-site

Workdays

Regular:
- Weeding Wednesdays - Parents' coffee group
- Annual or semi-annual

Adopt-a-bed Garden Fairies

Weeding

Class outdoor learning assistant;

Be explicit about what you want them to do:
- Hand out supplies and materials
- Extra set of eyes
- Take kids to the restroom
- Small group leader
- Redirect distracted students

On call to pick up supplies

Teachers are teaching, no time to pick up supplies.
- Coordinate other volunteers
- Farm stand support
- Tool upkeep

Off-site

Coordinate ther volunteers

Wash gloves

Sort seeds

Start and tend transplants for classes

Outreach to local business sponsors

Letting Go for Learning

From August to June, teachers work to create structure and systems in their classroom so students are ready to learn. We work endlessly, tweaking and fine-tuning a balance between structure and flexibility, routine and creativity. So many factors can upset the harmony of these two disciplines within a classroom. Teachers are constantly on the lookout for potential imbalances to the energy in their students. This may require teachers to act as human mood-stabilizers to keep learning challenging, fun, organized, flexible, creative, flowing and accessible–all at once.

Traditional school models can uphold antiquated ideals that communicate to teachers that students must be calm, quiet, and serious for learning. Although we now know that in student-centered learning we must provide opportunities for students to move, talk and explore, teachers are still under pressure to maintain a silent and studious atmosphere that does not in fact benefit many of our students. In effect, it is understandable if student behavior in outdoor learning is overwhelming at first. All of your hard work to instill values of respect, attention and self-control seems to disappear into thin air! This is often the moment when teachers can have big negative reactions with students to regain their expected level of control, or swear off teaching outdoors because students "can't handle it."

There is another choice at this moment. Take a deep breath and let go for learning. Look at what students are doing and saying:

Are they having fun and following safety rules for recess?

Are students exploring and talking about nature?

Are students stepping outside their comfort zone and trying new things?

Are they curious about the world around them and asking questions?

Outdoor learning is a wonderful medium between classroom behavior and play that provides opportunities for engagement, processing, and connection not possible within the walls of a school.

Learning outdoors looks different than in the classroom. Students behave differently because they are interacting with nature. This is a good thing! Outdoor time is a natural mood booster and will energize and engage students in a way not possible inside a school. Regardless of how many times students have heard expectations, these can be thrown to the wayside in outdoor learning space. Students talk louder, make bigger movements, and have bigger emotional reactions. Students seem distracted and interrupt you because the sun peeks out from behind a cloud, a bird chirps, and a bug buzzes by their ear. Alternatively, students can appear to be ignoring directions when they are actually completely absorbed in their experience. Might you have to momentarily cede the spotlight to a roly-poly that wanders onto a student's shoe?

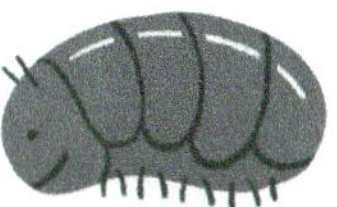

The answer is *yes!*

Nature has a limitless supply of sensory experiences for students. Often students read, write, and draw about plants, insects, and the natural elements without ever experiencing them firsthand. Outdoor learning finally makes these connections. Children now spend less time outside than any other previous generation. For many, a garden is full of completely new and different explorations. Just know, it's not you, it's nature!

Outdoor education can be a game changer for academic engagement and students' interests in science and the natural world. It is important that students have positive experiences in outdoor learning, even if behavior looks different than inside the classroom. In our sections Top Ten Tips for Great Outdoor Lessons and Setting Expectations and Guidelines for Fun and Safety you will find support on how to plan outdoor lessons with these factors in mind. Remember to embrace the joy and wonder of your students, and let go for learning!

© 2023 Partners for Education, Agriculture, and Sustainability

<h1 style="text-align:center">PEAS' Top Ten Tips
for Great Outdoor Lessons</h1>

1   Circle Up

Circles allow everyone to see, hear, and communicate that everyone is important. A great way to circle up is to gather around a natural object for study or demonstration.

2   Face the Sun

If you face the sun when you are outside, your audience won't have to.

3   Set Ground Rules

Set expectations for how to interact with rocks, sticks, and living things while you are outside. Suggestion: Ask students what they think! We've had success asking students:

- "What do you think a safe way to pick up a stick is?"
- "If we have a stick, what do we need to do to be safe?"
- "If we see a rock we want to pick up, how can we do it safely?"
- "If we see a beautiful flower, how could we enjoy it without harming it?"
- "If we see a spider, how could we respond while respecting the spider?"

More often than not, students have appropriate suggestions for how to be respectful and safe outdoors. If you ask for their input, you are co-creating the outdoor expectations.

4   Model the Ground Rules

- "I see a bee is flying around, but I know that bee doesn't want to sting me, so I'm going to be very calm and just observe it. Oh, now that bee is still buzzing around me, maybe I smell just like a flower, so I'm going to calmly move away."
- "I see a beautiful flower! I'm not going to pick the flower, because then it would die and wouldn't be able to provide nectar and habitat and beauty for our outdoor space, but I can get very close to it and use my senses to observe. It smells so nice! Up close I can see so many different parts! If I am very gentle, I can use one finger to feel how soft the petal is! Does anyone want to demonstrate how to gently observe this flower?"

5 Help Students Ground Themselves

Being outdoors can mean different things to different people. Some students will feel very comfortable sitting on the ground, and others will feel like ants are as scary as grizzly bears. A good technique to help students feel grounded is the 5-4-3-2-1 sensory countdown. This helps students calm any fight-or-flight response.

Coach them to note:

- 5 things they can see
- 4 things they can feel
- 3 things they can hear
- 2 things they can smell
- 1 thing they can taste (or just have them imagine eating a lemon. Once salivary glands kick in, the fight-or-flight response is short circuited.)

6 Set Boundaries Before Release

If you are going to allow students to explore or run, set boundaries. For younger students, consider touching each boundary or pointing out visual landmarks to show each boundary. "For this game/exploration, the boundaries are this tree, that chain-link fence, the edge of the track, and the bush with purple flowers." Have students point to each boundary and to where they will meet you when it is time to gather.

7 Help Release Pent-Up Energy

THE SHOUTING GAME

This is a good time to allow students to use their "outside voices" if they have been practicing using their "inside voices" in the classroom. One fun way to channel yelling is to use a ball or some object you can toss. Tell them that any time the object leaves your hands, they have to yell, but when it returns back to your hands, they have to stop.

LET IT OUT

Line students up at a starting line, allowing them to take one deep breath. On the exhale they will start to run and can run for as long as they can yell. This is a great way to release some energy before or after an activity that requires focus or sitting still.

8 Be Open to the Teachable Moments

Outdoor interruptions can become memorable moments! That hawk that flew overhead? Pause and notice it with your students! Do you know what bird that is? What did we observe about it? What color was its tail? Eyes? The butterfly that lands on your students head and pulls focus while you're explaining? Observe it! Congratulate your student for being still enough to let it land. Ask can you feel its feet? How heavy is it? Where did it come from? Where do you think it's going? Once you feel their interest dissipate, bring them back to the lesson.

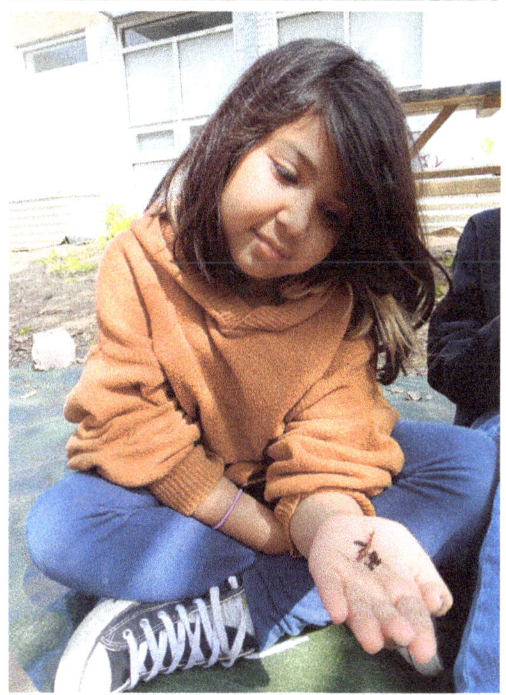

© 2023 Partners for Education, Agriculture, and Sustainability

9 Be a Conduit, Not a "Can't-Do-It"

Are your students digging a hole right in the middle of the garden, en-dangering the baby vegetables? Is there a different place where they could safely dig a hole? Instead of making a rule to not dig holes, consider helping them think through where they might be able to dig without hurting the outdoor area.

- "If you find a spot where you think you can dig safely, who should you ask first?" (The teacher)

- "What lives underground that we may need to be careful of?" (Roots, insects, worms)

- "How can we dig to protect our eyes and clothes and our friends' eyes and clothes?" (Carefully, not throwing dirt)

- "What should we do when we are done with our soil investigation?" (Replace all the dirt so no one trips and the underground living things have their habitat)

Poof! You've transformed "off-task behavior" into a self-guided soil investi-gation and embedded Leave No Trace principles.

10 Be Comfortable Not Knowing

Inevitably, students will ask you to identify birds, bugs, and plants. Allow your relationship to be more naturalist than expert. Engage students in observation and thinking about how they could find an answer. Invite them to make up their own names for plants (as this is what someone did with both common names and scientific names). Remind them that there are many, many organisms that have not been studied or discovered, and they, as observers, could easily discover something new.

More Ideas for Crafting Fun, Engaging, and Safe Lessons:

- **Best practices** in outdoor education recommend a 1:10 adult-to-student ratio. This is not always possible, so here are a few ways to help ensure fun and safety for all!

- **Recruit a volunteer** (parent, school mentor, local university students, or friend) to come in one day a week/month to assist with outdoor Set up centers for small groups of students to rotate through.

- **Team teach:** Some teachers temporarily reduce class size by making reciprocal arrangements with other teachers to take half of their class for a different lesson. (Be sure to repeat the project, this time permitting the other half of the class to participate.)

- **Buddy classes:** Another variation on team teaching that also includes aspects of cooperative learning is a "buddy class" system that teams a lower grade class with an upper grade, matching students one-on-one for projects. Each teacher works with half of both classes at once.

- **Start simple:** The first lesson of the year should be something simple like a scavenger hunt to get students familiar with their surroundings and help them to learn the rules and boundaries.

- **Build in a written, oral, or art-based activity for each lesson.** Charts, lists, graphic organizers, illustrations, paintings, model building, and round robin reflections are a great way to assess whether students are making connections to the lesson outside.

- **Set up centers** for small groups of students to rotate through.

- **Anticipate distractions** and plan accordingly. Students may not be able to stay focused on the lesson when the preschoolers are having their track and field day.

- **Provide tools:** Rulers, string for measuring, magnifying glasses, egg cartons for collections, cups for watering, and bug catchers are a great way for students to hold on to an object that can help them focus on the objective.

- **Make a base:** Find an area to designate as base. Tell students by the time you countdown from 10-0 they should all be back on base, ready to listen to the next set of instructions.

- **Bring blankets:** Students often need somewhere to sit while writing and making observations and will be more comfortable if they are not in the grass or dirt. (Blankets or tarps make great bases.)

© 2023 Partners for Education, Agriculture, and Sustainability

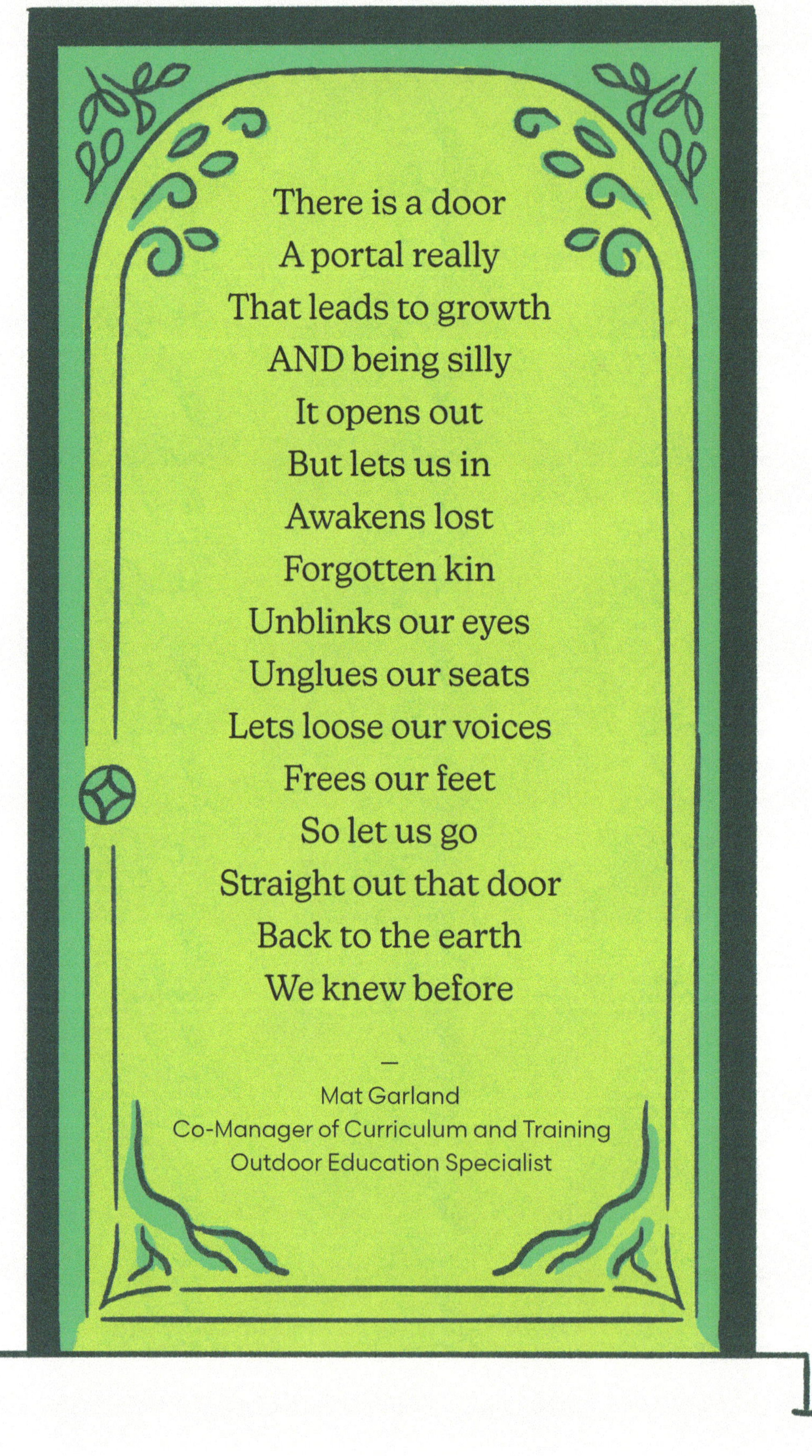
There is a door
A portal really
That leads to growth
AND being silly
It opens out
But lets us in
Awakens lost
Forgotten kin
Unblinks our eyes
Unglues our seats
Lets loose our voices
Frees our feet
So let us go
Straight out that door
Back to the earth
We knew before

—
Mat Garland
Co-Manager of Curriculum and Training
Outdoor Education Specialist

Why Outdoor Education?

BY ERIN MAGRATH

There may come a time when the benefits and impact of learning outdoors are called into question by different stakeholders in your educational community. Here you will find research-based evidence which highlights the many physical, psychological, and academic advantages of garden and outdoor education which justify these essential experiences for all of our students and teachers.

In this section, we illustrate the many benefits of outdoor education, and explore why intentional and robust outdoor engagement is crucial for the physical, psychological, and academic future of our students. Like a garden, outdoor education requires careful planting of partnerships for diverse and reciprocal systems of support. The curriculum of outdoor learning respects, honors, and celebrates the land with a social justice, equity, and activist lens. When growing young minds, educators listen to students and center learning in their identities and stories. We must maintain a flexible and resilient mindset because when teaching, especially in outdoor spaces, we are at the whim of living and nonliving elements. We learn and reflect from these experiences; we are open to critique so as to move forward with our important work.

In the past decades, schools have been slowly closing their walls around our students, especially our populations impacted most by structural racism and discrimination, and limiting their experiences and connection to the outdoors. Teachers and faculty feel pressure to limit experiences outdoors because of insurmountable to-do lists, unrealistic expectations, and perpetual testing cycles which seem to increase yearly. Other factors which contribute to less time spent outdoors are long hours worked by parents, increasingly extreme weather conditions, lack of vegetation in urban heat islands, and the irresistible pull of technology in our youngest generations. United States children today spend less time outdoors than any previous generation, spending three times as many hours playing on the computer or watching television than playing outside (Lanza et al., 2021). Nature-deficit disorder, first labeled and identified by Richard Louv, is a condition where reduced experiences outdoors and in natural spaces negatively affect the educational development and emotional health of children (Louv, 2005). For the physical and emotional health of our youngest generation, we must provide safe and engaging opportunities to learn outdoors.

Never has it been more crucial for schools to provide explicit experiences for students to learn, work, and explore outdoors. School administrations may argue that students receive sufficient time for these pastimes during recess; however, our children and future Earthkeepers deserve engaging, academically rich instruction to develop a relationship with the outdoors. We must cultivate a generation that is deeply invested in the welfare of our planet, with a respect and wonder for nature that greatly surpasses the attitudes of our current world leaders. Outdoor education can inspire environmental stewardship and advocacy in students. Teachers must engage students in concrete experiences paired with explicit discussions about environmental care (Roberts et al. 2021, p. 53). Divergent thinking, creativity, and collaboration are foundational practices of outdoor education and will be the practices of our future global community.

We must uphold students' identities and engage their families with their learning in schools and our greater natural environment. Schools can accomplish these community-centered goals through outdoor and gardening education. However, there are challenges and fossilized thinking which must be overcome in order to cultivate these opportunities for our future generations. We must bravely push through fears of change and shift the paradigm toward authentic student learning and Earth-centered education for the welfare of our children and our planet.

Commitment to Equity, Social Justice, and Environmental Justice

For many years there has been a movement to separate education from nature and agriculture as an intentional erasure of our involvement and unbreakable connection with the Earth. Our way back to crucial human practices of respect, honor, and stewardship of our spaces shared with other living beings must be through a restorative, social, and environmental justice framework.

Since the birth of public education, students have been slowly weaned from nature, playing outdoors, and agricultural practices through the narrative that success, intelligence, and learning can only happen indoors through sedentary study.

© 2023 Partners for Education, Agriculture, and Sustainability

While many successes have been achieved in this manner, this narrative has also excluded and shamed learners from agricultural backgrounds, those who have naturalist or spatial intelligences, or individuals who thrive upon experiential learning in nature. Our society has proclaimed that individuals who desire to work outdoors and in nature are of less value than those who choose indoor professions. In the process, we severed many students' connections with their families, history, and innate belonging as children to the natural world. In the United States, many young children, especially those in families experiencing economic hardship and urban populations, do not have access to safe green spaces, and opportunities to be outdoors are reduced. For these reasons, outdoor education must start with equity and social justice to reawaken our kinship in nature. Outdoor education returns to the harmonious practices of past generations like growing your own food, respecting nature, and building symbiotic relationships with all living beings. These practices are where true power and interdependence are found within our communities.

Outdoor education must center lessons with culturally relevant teachings, continual training around antiracist multicultural practices, and inclusion of Indigenous histories and present-day cultures. When we honor the innovations, traditions, and beliefs of an array of cultures and groups, we give students an opportunity to feel belonging within our curriculum. Culturally responsive and student-centered education in a garden or outdoor space is an important part of our relationship to the outdoors and our shared history. Outdoor lessons with a decolonizing framework root learning in environmental and social justice.

Professional development and workplace collaborative projects for outdoor education must emphasize dismantling racist and neo-colonialist practices within agriculture. When outdoor educators learn and acknowledge the history and people of the lands where they teach, there is an ability to initiate restorative practices and social action. When teachers understand the inequities of their community, they can authentically focus their energies toward social justice and environmentally restorative practices.

Benefits of Outdoor Education

Outdoor education ranges from learning core subjects outside, to environmentally focused lessons in outdoor spaces, to learning how to garden through agricultural lessons. Our work is place-based and rooted in the community of the learners and educators. Outdoor education provides a holistic offering of advantages to the well-being of our students, such as physical, academic, and psychological benefits.

PHYSICAL BENEFITS

Increased access to the natural spaces, along with educational development in outdoor and garden environments, improves the physical activity level and nutritional choices of children. In fact, time spent outdoors is one of the most consistently positive correlations of physical activity among children (Rees-Punia et al., 2017, p. 959). An English study, Project WHY, monitored the activity levels, specifically their moderate to vigorous physical activity (MVPA) of students, through accelerometers. During outdoor learning students spent a significantly larger portion of their learning at MVPA activity levels than indoor learning situations. Observational data in Project WHY showed that students developed gross and fine motor skills and that outdoor learning sessions had a positive effect on their physical well-being (Waite & Arronson, 2022). Researchers found that gardening is a promising strategy to improve children's dietary habits (Evans et al. 2016, p. 619). In one study, students from 28 different schools with a high number of families experiencing economic hardship in Texas received gardening lessons over several months of the school year. After several lessons, students were asked if they enjoyed gardening and if they would like to eat more fruit and vegetables. Students who enjoyed gardening ate significantly more fruits and vegetables than before the study. Even students who responded that they did not like their gardening classes had an increased interest in consuming fruits and vegetables (Evans et al., 2016).

Research shows that, along with improving the current health of our student community, time spent outdoors may prevent long-term and chronic ailments. Time spent outdoors, especially gardening for young people and adults alike, is a well-known practice to lower blood pressure and improve mobility and cardiovascular health. Also known as the "sunshine vitamin," vitamin D is absorbed through skin from sunlight. Vitamin D strengthens the immune system, prevents certain cancers, boosts your mood, and lowers the risk of type 2 diabetes. Absorption is more difficult for populations with darker skin tones, as higher amounts of melanin in the skin prevent the cellular production of vitamin D. One study found that 61% of otherwise healthy Black and Hispanic adolescents had low vitamin D levels, which dropped even lower with age (Fickman, 2022).The study called for awareness and further investigations, citing that the cause for vitamin D deficiencies could be social determinants such as education, social, and community context. Due to impacts of structural racism many of our students who would benefit more time outdoors for their long-term health are unable to access safe spaces and extended amounts of time outdoors. Outdoor education provides the opportunity for students to be outside and develop a relationship with the outdoors, so they may benefit from its many preventive advantages for years to come.

The process of participating in an agricultural process is powerful for young children, as they feel accomplishment and responsibility toward their crops and can use their hands to touch, smell, and taste their own hard work. A more connected experience with gardening and outdoor exploration inspires a curiosity toward healthy choices. Cultivating a love for the outdoors can have short- and long-term health benefits for our students.

PSYCHOLOGICAL BENEFITS

Quality Outdoor Education programs have many mental health benefits for students and promote a child's innate connection to nature and belonging.

Natasha Etherton's book, Gardening for Children with Spectrum Disorders and Special Educational Needs, states engaging with nature provides a trifecta of opportunities to build social skills, promote sensory integration, and alleviate anxiety (2012). Children spend more time indoors than any previous generation. More young people are experiencing Nature-deficit disorder which causes higher rates of physical and emotional illnesses along with reduced use of senses and attention disorders (Louv, 2015). Furthermore, many children, especially individuals on the neurodivergent spectrum (includes children with dyslexia, ADHD, or on the spectrum of autism) can experience anxiety in a traditional school setting. These learners feel empowered to apply their range of neurodivergent traits such as creative and innovative thinking, concentration and observation skills, and empathy with ease in outdoor spaces. Outdoor education can support these students through hands-on, multisensory learning in a natural space. Students with an ADHD label were more focused and showed greater achievement after spending time learning

outdoors (Rees-Punia et al. 2017). Gardening and agricultural education was found to boost the mood of students and has been proven to have long lasting effects in combating anxiety and depression (Rees-Punia et al., 2017).

Collaboration and teamwork are large components of outdoor education, and students strengthen their cooperative and social skills through outdoor learning (Lucas, 2018). Gardens and outdoor spaces also provide children an opportunity to connect with each other through exploration, growing food, and experiencing nature together. Teachers with experience in outdoor learning emphasized the role of these outdoor spaces in the social development of the children (Austin, 717).

Outdoor learning creates a wealth of opportunities for our students with learning disabilities, mental health struggles, and behavior issues. These are the students who most need the opportunity to run, spin and jump like their favorite insect, break a sweat weeding a raised bed garden, or be given a full five minutes to observe a ladybug on a tree. Students who struggle inside the classroom can often flourish and shine outdoors.

The benefits of outdoor learning don't stop with the students. It has been reported that even a couple of hours a week outdoors with students can elevate job satisfaction of teachers. (An hour or two of outdoor learning every week increases teachers' job satisfaction, 1999).

ACADEMIC BENEFITS

Students spend time in outdoor education scenarios and develop a great interest and empathy for natural elements, living organisms, and the well-being of our planet. The global climate crisis is felt in virtually all communities on our planet, and we must work to promote a deep sense of environmental stewardship in our students through positive outdoor learning experiences. School gardens provide an opportunity for even our youngest students to learn academic content and ecological awareness. One study found that second grade students who were afraid of bugs and complained about getting dirt on their hands began to protect these same animals and enjoyed digging in the dirt after lessons gardening and exploring their garden space (Fisher-Maltese, 2016). If we hope for future generations to collaborate in creating solutions for our climate crisis, we must instill them with the values of reciprocity and reverence for the environment. David Sobel exemplified this sentiment when he said, "If we want children to flourish to become truly empowered, then let us allow them to love the earth before we ask them to save it." (Sobel, 1999, p.47).

Outdoor learning can uphold cultural belonging and connection to home cultures in school settings. Many students have families who grow plants or have a connection to farming and feel a connection to their family in school garden spaces. Students have opportunities to be experts and uphold their family members as sources of knowledge and expertise. When

© 2023 Partners for Education, Agriculture, and Sustainability

exploring the herb garden with kindergarten students, one PEAS student proclaimed, "Ya sé esta hierba es la hierbabuena! Se la toma cuando estás mal de estómago, mi mamá me la prepara en un té cuando no me siento bien. A mí me gusta como huele." (Translation: "This herb is spearmint! You take it when you have a stomachache. My Mommy prepares it for me in a tea when I don't feel good. I like how it smells.") Pride and confidence beamed out of the child's face as she connected the knowledge of her mother to our garden lesson and demonstrated her expertise and belonging.

As we expand ecological awareness among ourselves and our students, we do not discount the narratives of systemic oppression that may dissuade communities from engaging in outdoor and agricultural practices. Many communities remain disenfranchised due to systems of oppression tied to agriculture, land, and labor. We are motivated to be pillars of trust empowering sovereign choice and providing opportunities so that each child may experience a sense of freedom as they connect with the natural world. It is our great privilege to not only serve diverse communities, but to also amplify a multitude of environmental stewards from various cultural backgrounds, within our organization and beyond. In the words of environmental activist Vandana Shiva, cultural diversity creates the conditions for peace (Shiva, 2015, p.8). We seek to promote a sense of dignity of this essential work and deep connection to the Earth. Remembering we are Earth citizens and Earth children can help us recover our common humanity (Shiva, 2015, p. 6).

Many new shifts will happen in the educational landscape in the years to come, and outdoor education should be counted as a dynamic and multifaceted avenue to provide accessible and rigorous learning. Students in outdoor education lessons showed higher engagement in science lessons; older students took an interest in fields of study in environmental protection and activist professions (Graves et al., 2016). One study concluded that outdoor education had a positive effect on the students' level of remembering their knowledge (memory retention and recall) and permanent learning in comparison to their peers who received only indoor instruction of the same content. (Avic & Nevzat, 2020). Outdoor learning and gardening education often elicits the use of multiple intelligences. First pioneered by Michael Gardner, the theory of multiple intelligences asserts that people have a diverse set of talents and abilities which affect their preferred learning style. Researchers Tabari and Tabari utilized Gardner's eight intelligences and coded them to Bloom's taxonomy, a widely known hierarchy of cognitive processing used as the basis for classroom lesson planning. They found that apart from linguistic intelligences, all other intelligences (and ways we can connect to our students and their strengths) were woefully underrepresented (Tabari & Tabari, 2015). In the study, we see the inequity and exclusion of students where only select intelligences (mainly literacy and math) are valued and rewarded. Hands-on, sensory activities of free exploration and inquiry or lessons which integrate the core subjects through nature

and agriculture can access students' kinesthetic, naturalist, intrapersonal, and extrapersonal intelligences. A quiet, non participatory student might engage through extraordinary observational skills of nature. A kinesthetic learner can excel at a dance representing the pollinators species in a garden. A student with naturalist intelligence could discover a lifelong passion for farming and the environment. Reawakening the wisdom and lessons that come with outdoor learning is so important for students who thrive in the natural world. Outdoor education awakens curiosity, inclusive learning opportunities, and environmental consciousness in our students.

Conclusion

Outdoor Education is a powerful instrument for children's academic and psychological development and an important tool for our uncertain environmental future. We must push through the challenges of our changing world and provide students with restorative and academically engaging outdoor experiences. Outdoor learning programs, whether a single teacher's efforts or a district-wide initiative, can find creative solutions for the many challenges that face our work. Together, we can return students to the wonder and exploration of nature, to build a healthy, equitable, and inclusive future.

Much of this section came from the graduate-level research project of Erin Magrath, Co-Manager of Curriculum and Training.

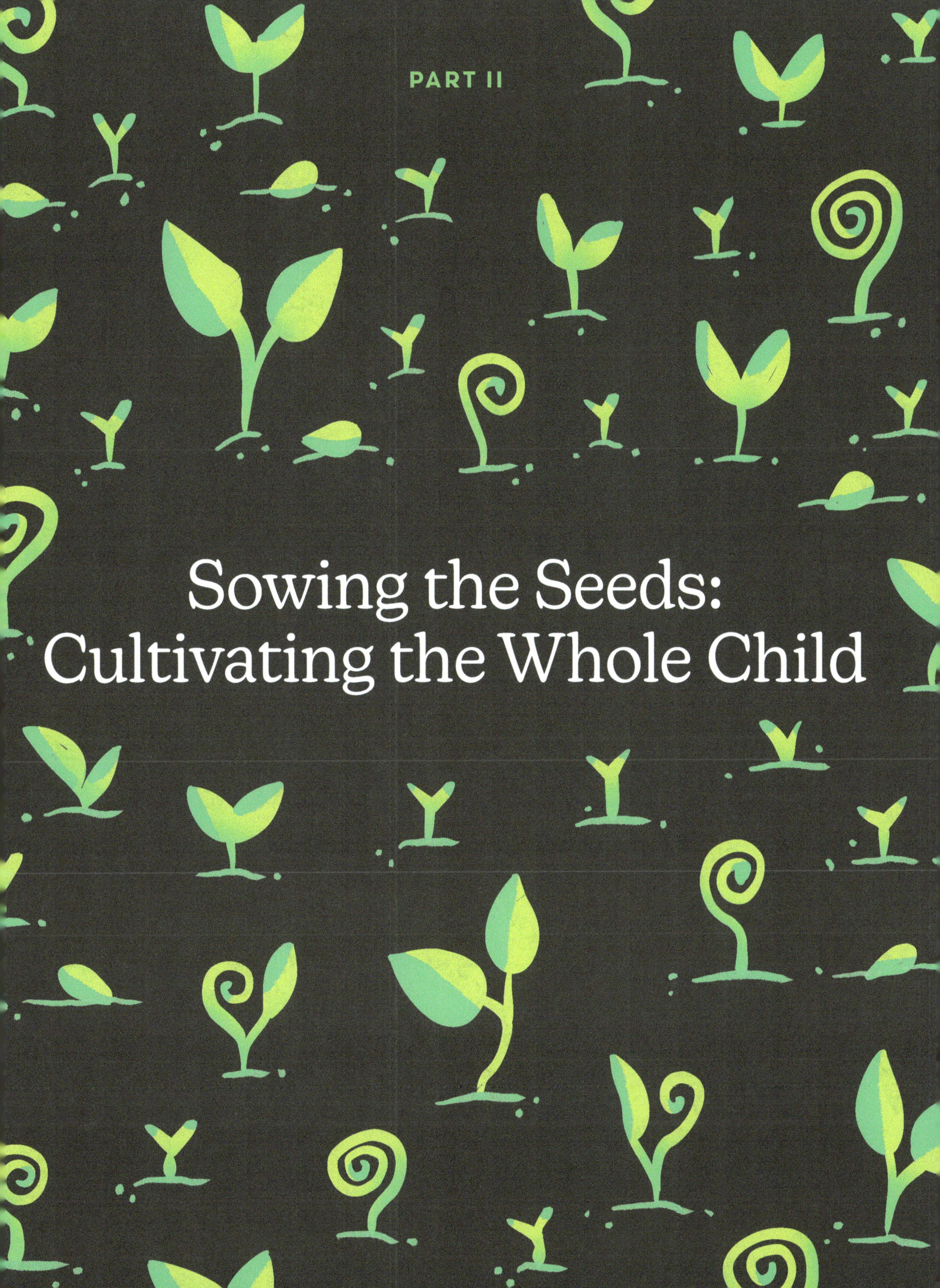

Sowing the Seeds: Cultivating the Whole Child

Opportunities to Honor the Earth

> "Action on behalf of life transforms.
> Because the relationship between self
> and the world is reciprocal, it is not a
> question of first getting enlightened or
> saved and then acting.
>
> As we work to heal the earth,
> the earth heals us."

— ROBIN WALL KIMMERER, *BRAIDING SWEETGRASS*

As facilitators of learning, we take our classes outside to experience connection. We hold space for our students to build relationships with living and nonliving aspects within our natural world. We open opportunities for children to heal from the stress of modern society. We know that for our mental, emotional, cognitive, and physical health, we need more time following ladybugs in the garden and less time filling in multiple choice bubbles. At PEAS, all of our work is deeply rooted in honoring the Earth.

The essences of our beings crave connections to each other and among the other beings and elements (rocks, water, fire) of our natural world. The more we pull away from growing these integral and inherent relationships, the more we feel lost and question our being. The vast history of human development involved close interaction with the natural world. Our air-conditioned and plugged-in modern society has disconnected many from the outdoors. There is much research showing the negative impacts of this separation. That's why taking learning outdoors is more important today than it ever was in the past.

When we commune with the elements of Earth, we understand the reciprocity that Robin Wall Kimmerer mentions in the quote above because we have direct experience of the relationships. When students explore the relationships in nature, they begin to understand their own place in these systems. In turn, they experience the reciprocity of nature through the air we breathe, the water we drink, and the food we eat. We are all members of the greater ecosystem we call Earth. Students need time and opportunities to integrate this wisdom.

Since the beginning, public education has been bound in a system of oppression. As educators, so many of us are looking for opportunities to decolonize our practice. Instead of moving our antiquated teaching narratives outside, let's expand and restore the definition of how we connect and learn. Outdoor education is a great place to start reintroducing Indigenous ways of teaching, learning, and being. The opportunities for storytelling, building community, communing with other natural beings, and celebrating multicultural narratives are vital and limitless.

When outdoor education centers around food gardens, our opportunities increase even further. What better way to learn about the abundance and diversity of cultures across the globe than through food? When we include traditions from all families in our school communities by sharing stories while cooking together, we learn life skills and cultivate academic competencies.

In choosing to move classes outdoors and increase connectivity with nature and food, we are not only crafting lasting connections for our students, but for ourselves as well. As we uplift the kinship between ourselves, children, and the Earth, we unfurl an offering of honor towards the natural world.

I see the child in me
Twirling, spiraling
Down to the questions asked
Up to the wishes granting passed
I see the teacher within me
Cradling, guiding
Out from the heartaches
Into our journey to Reawaken

—

Lauren Reneé Salinas-Garcia
Outdoor Education Specialist

© 2023 Partners for Education, Agriculture, and Sustainability

Honor Kinship, Elevate Earthkeepers

BY LAUREN RENÉE SALINAS-GARCIA

This passage is an offering to new and seasoned educators alike. My name is Lauren Reneé Salinas-Garcia. I was born where the marvelous springs of the San Marcos River still flow. My ancestors, relatives and I are Indigenous to what are known today as Texas and Mexico. Despite the fragmentation inflicted upon Indigenous knowledge, language, and cultural traditions, deep connection to the spirit of nature sustains resilience and continues to grow and impact my life in profound ways. In my journey of reclaiming my indigeneity and connecting to my heritage through ancient practices, I find that my multicultural ethnic and urban background empowers me as an educator to serve a diverse community of students. My background deeply informs my work as an Earthkeeper and Outdoor Education Specialist. It is my personal mission to celebrate, elevate, and fortify the sacred connection between Black and Indigenous communities and children with the natural world.

In 2019, I began my journey in homesteading: foraging seasonal fruits; keeping guinea fowl and chickens; deepening my knowledge of plant identification; and tending a small community garden. My awareness of myself as the only woman of color in the developing eco-village community where I resided further ignited my personal mission. I often felt the sting of inequity and noticed the misalignment of values and the omission of diversity and inclusion. Experiences such as mine are but a mere fractal of a macrocosmic issue. It is important to address the deprecation of accreditation, lack of representation, and hindrance to amplify BIPOC voices and value in the "environmentalist" space. However, I am hopeful that our work, along with others, will further instill self-efficacy in young children to endeavor toward initiatives, careers, and missions that will uplift the intersections of environmentalism.

That same year, I began a Teacher's Assistant position at Zavala Elementary in historic East Austin, Texas. Here is where I witnessed the PEAS program in action and was inspired by how the organization's mission aligned with my own. I loved seeing young students learn about composting, harvest carrots, taste rosemary, and connect with trees. My childhood dreams were unfurling like butterfly wings right before my eyes! I would later transition into Zavala Elementary's very own PEAS Outdoor Education Specialist.

What I love about PEAS is the many ways our students experience the natural world and other living beings as friends. Companionship is a vital aspect of my personal approach to cultivating a deeper sense of appreciation and respect toward nature. I have witnessed how this ancient way of relating to the natural world empowers empathy within my students toward outdoor environments as ecosystems. I also see how they experience a sense of wonder, play, and genuine reverence when we are together. It is truly a gift to bear witness to my students' blossoming as fellow Earthkeepers.

In order to gain a deeper sense of how children will learn with PEAS, I put myself in the perspective of the learner. In this way, I experience many moments of mindful engagement with our students! It is my privilege now to offer a glimpse into some of the ways we honor the Earth in PEAS lessons. To start, gathering in a circle allows me to feel more connected with my students. When I greet my students for the day, I invite them to hug their own bodies. "Open up your arms, give yourself a big hug," I say. "Because you are lovable, just like our garden!" Love is a major component of our work! We express affection to ourselves, just as we do to the earthworms, ladybugs, trees, seeds, and water.

We often speak to the trees and offer them hugs in many outdoor environments. When we add a fresh layer of compost for the Oak Trees, we take time to hold the soil and think kindly toward the tree. Together we sprinkle the compost of good thoughts to the soil. My kindergarten students enjoy sharing their thoughts with me. I hear things like "I told the tree I missed her and that I love her!"; "I told the tree she is beautiful!"; and "I told the tree thank you for being our friend!"

When it is time to plant new crops, I place seeds in my students' hands and invite my students to interact with them. "You may hug your seeds in your hand. You could hold them to your heart. Maybe think a happy thought or say some nice words like, 'I hope you grow big and strong!'" Before planting, we lift seeds up to the sun and say, "Thank you, friend!" Sometimes we pass an unopened seed packet around our circle so everyone can shake them and cheer, "Go carrots, go carrots!" We believe all of our energy transmutes into growing happy, healthy plants.

Respecting the life and the needs of the growing plants is important to my students. We "pour low and slow to the roots in the soil." We ask ourselves, "Is this plant safe for eating?" "Is there enough for this plant to share before we harvest?" To encourage reciprocity and symbiosis, we offer plants water, so that we are also nurturing toward them, thanking them as we harvest. Before tasting new herbs or vegetables, I remind my students that just as the plant is a part of nature, so are we. I ask "Do we want to say unkind words to ourselves or about nature?" "No!" They all respond. "So let's do our best to speak kindly to the plants. If the taste is not for you, say 'not for me' and return it to the earth for composting." This has helped many of my students feel a sense of pride toward the food they grow, broaden their horizons of taste, and build upon respect toward food. When it is time to part ways for the day, I thank my students for their presence, for their care toward their gardens, and for respecting the environment. They usually depart by blowing kisses and waving goodbye to the trees, plants, flowers, and their outdoor classrooms.

In order to enrich my responsibility as an educator, I persistently meditate on how my ancestors in centuries past would have shared their Earth connections and imparted knowledge to me. Through these reflections and practices, I have experienced so much joy with my students, as a teacher and as an infinite learner. I sincerely believe that many of our students are connecting with the natural world in a very potent and expansive way. My highest honor is as a guide, witnessing children's joy and wonder as we cultivate our kinship with the natural world.

© 2023 Partners for Education, Agriculture, and Sustainability

Background for Trauma-Informed Instruction

Trauma-informed instruction is the care, compassion, and acceptance of students regardless of their successes or failures in an educational setting. Students coping with trauma may experience sudden, unexpected behavior changes because of ongoing or past situations in which their safety has been threatened. Trauma can have significant negative consequences upon the academic progress and the social emotional development of students. Trauma-informed instructional practices seek to implement strategic responses which provide safe spaces for students and allow them to practice emotional self-regulation skills. Educators learn about different trauma responses. in order to be able to confidently and compassionately address behaviors from a nonjudgmental and caring perspective

Addressing Traumatic Experiences with Nature and the Outdoors

After a traumatic experience in an outdoor environment, it can take time to rebuild confidence and trust with any space that might trigger dysregulating thoughts and feelings. The type of situation matters little (it may be something as common as a bee sting or intense as violence or a migration experience) because our brains process and heal from past situations in different ways. Furthermore, students may inherit intergenerational trauma where outdoor and wild spaces are regarded with fear and mistrust. As you introduce your class to new outdoor learning experiences, establish open lines of communication with your students about how they are feeling. If you know that a student is triggered by an outdoor space, opening these opportunities slowly and intentionally to them will help create a foundation of trust for future learning.

While we cannot completely assure students that accidents will never occur, we can form trust-based relationships with our classroom community so students may feel supported to process and ask for what they need in moments of stress. Educators provide space for students to feel and work in different ways, as seen here from one of our partner teachers while working with one of her students:

"This school year, I had a scholar who came from a rural community in Honduras. Some of her siblings were still there, as well as her grandmother.

When we spent time in the garden, she would be reminded of how her family had a *milpa* [small farm] where they harvested their food from. Sometimes she would be very happy to be there, and other times she would be very pensive and quiet. The other kids would notice.

When I asked if she was okay, she would tell me about her family and how she worried about them in Honduras because it was not safe for them there."

Let's facilitate the growth and healing of our students by providing supportive, trust-based communication so they may repair their relationship with the outdoors.

Why Is Trauma-Informed Instruction Relevant to Outdoor Learning?

In an outdoor setting, trauma-informed instructional strategies are an important skill set. Outdoor learning adds a layer of engagement and joy to the educational experience, but it also comes with potential fears and triggers for certain students. Student safety, compliance, and focus look different outdoors. Teachers must discern students who are excitedly engaging with their outdoor environment versus students making dysregulated choices. Expectations and teacher behavior are also modified accordingly so that educators themselves stay regulated in outdoor learning (read more about this in Setting Expectations and Guidelines for Fun and Safety and Letting Go for Learning).

The heightened sensory experience of outdoor learning may be a trigger for students. Whether the change in temperature, the feel of a prickly stick, a sudden appearance of a flying insect, or the feel of sweat and thirst, students can be triggered into trauma response. Especially during initial outdoor learning experiences with a class, teachers must identify the triggers of students and respond with compassion and patience.

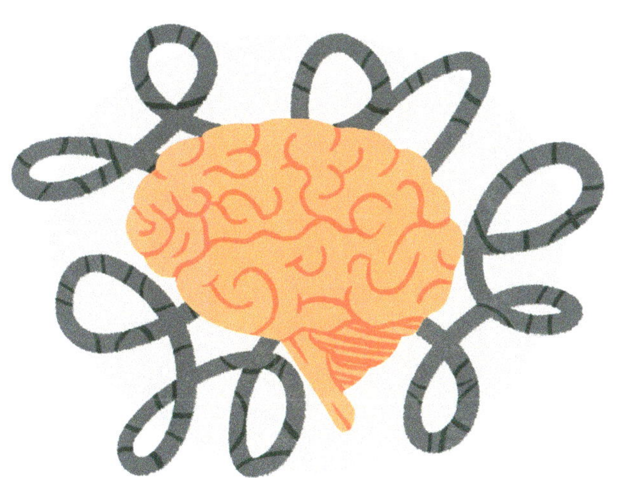

Guide to Trauma Responses

A crucial element of trauma-informed instruction establishes that trauma responses are not all the same. A student's response to trauma activates in different parts of the brain and requires varied strategies. Behaviors signaling a dysregulated student can be tied to their executive, emotional, or survival state of functioning. A teacher must notice and discern these different trauma responses in order to effectively and thoughtfully support their student.

All trauma responses communicate to teachers that the student is in need of help. This communication may present as noncompliant, aggressive, or disrespectful choices. Our job as educators is to regulate our own emotions in order to assess the needs of our students. An effective strategy to support and understand the needs of a student is to always lead from a noticing versus judging mindset.

Noticing Versus Judging

The thought process and speech of an educator when interacting with a distressed student can greatly influence the outcome and resolution of trauma response.

Judging students is when teachers intertwine our own dysregulated emotions with the choices of students. An educator may shame students and or punish them in order to exert control. Judgment based on punishments and speech communicates to students they are only worthy of love when they make good choices. When students are dysregulated, they cannot access the decision-making process. Judgment-based discipline is unfair and will perpetuate a student's self-image of being a "bad kid." Behavior management techniques based in control and forced compliance defer a solution and create long-term damage to the self-esteem of students. These tactics inhibit the mutual respect and trust needed for a cohesive and successful learning community.

When we notice a student's misbehavior, we refrain from attaching our own emotional response. A teacher who notices a student's behavior without judgment is able to move towards solutions-based actions that will support students to make better choices. Always assume positive intent with students. Know that students are using tools to meet their needs that they have learned in their development, and it is our responsibility to guide them to make different choices. When the child is regulated, teachers can introduce new strategies to help students navigate their emotions and build relationships;

© 2023 Partners for Education, Agriculture, and Sustainability

these crucial skills will help them throughout their lives. Compassionate, noticing teachers understand that students may live in difficult, unstable situations. Educators must be consistent, steady champions for children as they develop in a community of learners.

It can be difficult to distinguish between a noticing and judging mindset. Here are some examples in the context of Outdoor Education.

While reading the below examples, in the spirit of trauma-based instruction, please consider the following list with self-reflection, compassion, and grace.

Noticing: What is happening with the student?	**Judging:** What is happening with me?
Student is not looking at me but playing with grass as I give directions.	Student is not listening to me. Student will slow down activity and cause issues.
Students are running when I said to walk.	Students are being disrespectful and I must control their behavior or we won't get our work done.
While teacher is talking, student interrupts and yells out.	Student is rude and not listening so will be unable to do activity.
Student refuses to sit with the group or work.	Student is being disrespectful and lazy — more will join in if I don't make them work.

Nourish the Heart and Minds of Students with Outdoor Education

There is an undeniable connection between children and the outdoors. The joy, curiosity, and organic learning of students outside is a testament to its incorporation within the school day. Children's experiences outdoors may be stressful and triggering. Teachers must understand how to ease the difficulty of this reintegration to the outdoors and move forward without judgment in order to bring joyful connections to the natural world for all students.

Holistic Benefits of Outdoor Learning

Bringing student learning outdoors can result in better academic outcomes by providing tangible and experiential learning opportunities. The benefits of outdoor education can also have positive physical and mental health outcomes. The following section explores how social and emotional wellness and physical health can be supported through bringing learning outside.

SEL Basics

Social and Emotional Learning (SEL) is the process in which students gain knowledge and skills to understand their identity, achieve their goals, and engage in their communities. According to CASEL (Collaborative for Academic, Social, and Emotional Learning), SEL has five competencies of **Self-Awareness, Self-Management, Social Awareness, Relationship Building,** and **Responsible Decision-Making.** These five areas help students understand themselves and others through empathy and a critical thinking approach. With a holistic approach, social and emotional learning can be implemented in the classrooms, schools, families, and communities of students. Strengthening the relationship between families, community, and schools is a key practice of SEL.

The Five Competencies of SEL

Self-Awareness develops the internal thoughts and feelings of students and their understanding of their culture. SEL facilitates skillful practices of **Self-Management** where students are able to understand and process their thoughts, feelings, and actions. **Social Awareness** teaches students about communities and cultures. This competency develops a sense of perspective and empathy toward other groups. In the **Relationship Building** competency, students learn to connect with others through effective communication and advocacy. **Responsible Decision-Making** helps students think critically about their relationships and role in the community in order to make good choices for themselves and others.

SEL Holistic Approach

SEL education can be present in all areas of student life. Within a classroom, students receive SEL-integrated instruction where academic content is taught through a social justice lens. Students practice empathy, collaboration, and mindfulness to achieve their academic goals.

SOCIAL & EMOTIONAL LEARNING: CORE COMPETENCIES

SELF-MANAGEMENT
Managing emotions and behaviors to achieve one's goals.

SELF-AWARENESS
Recognizing one's emotions and values as well as one's strengths and challenges.

SOCIAL AWARENESS
Showing understanding and empathy for others.

RELATIONSHIP SKILLS
Forming positive relationships, working in teams, dealing effectively with conflict.

RESPONSIBLE DECISION-MAKING
Making ethical, constructive choices about personal and social behavior.

(What is the CASEL Framework?, n.d.)

Schools implement SEL to create a welcoming and inclusive environment for all students. SEL-focused schools redesign behavior management to provide a safe and supportive environment which upholds the experience of all students. Family involvement in SEL creates a trust-based relationship between parents, schools, and community. Families engage students with strategies from the five core competencies to support their students outside of the classroom. Communities can use SEL to provide opportunities where students feel belonging and pride in their community. All areas of implementation for SEL help strengthen the identity and culture of students so they may achieve their personal goals and engage with their community.

Benefits of SEL

Social and emotional learning increases academic achievement and classroom behavior among students who receive well-implemented programming. SEL interventions enhance young peoples' emotional management skills and lower cases of depression and anxiety. SEL is beneficial among all demographic groups and supports the development of students from diverse backgrounds and geographic contexts.[1] Families, teachers, and students have called for greater emphasis on social and emotional learning. Postpandemic, 56% of teachers believe SEL will be the most critical skill for their students, and 90% of elementary and secondary teachers agreed that promoting SEL is beneficial to their students' achievement. Also, 62% of parents surveyed believe SEL to be very important, and 81% believe not enough SEL instruction is present in schools. The research shows that young people benefit widely from high-quality SEL instruction and intervention.[1]

Ecotherapy

The concept of ecotherapy, also known as nature therapy, centers on formal and informal therapeutic practices conducted outdoors. Formal Ecotherapy (sometimes written with a capital "E") is led by a trained mental health professional and has been shown to produce positive and lasting benefits. Examples of the activities used in ecotherapy sessions include meditation, wildlife exploration, nature journaling, animal interaction, gardening, and arts and crafts. Research done at the University of Michigan found that just 20 minutes a day in nature can significantly lower stress hormone levels.[2]

As teachers, we acknowledge that while we may not be trained mental health professionals, including therapeutic nature activities with our students can provide many positive outcomes. If you suspect a student needs mental health interventions, they should be referred for counseling. Using components of ecotherapy is not a replacement for formal counseling.

Forest Bathing

In the early 1980's the Japanese government began a program called shinrin-yoku (translated in English as "forest bathing") in response to high levels of work-related stress, depression, and rising rates of auto-immune disorders in many of its citizens. Dr. Yoshifumi Miyazaki, lead researcher on shinrin-yoku, wanted to harness the perceived positive feelings associated with exposure to nature as a tool in combating mental health issues.

Shinrin-yoku is based on a series of invitations led by a guide. Each invitation encourages the practitioner to focus deeply on their senses to connect with the natural world around them. Sessions are usually less than an hour and do not require a large natural space. Shinrin-yoku is not just a hike, but a focused series of connections to the natural world. By the late 1980's, researchers studying the effects of shinrin-yoku had documented strong correlations between these practices and improved health outcomes. Researchers measured heart rate, blood pressure, stress hormone levels, and immune system indicators and found tangible positive results. Japan has now established shinrin-yoku trails throughout the country and continues to research and promote the practice of forest bathing.

The benefits of forest bathing can be extrapolated to outdoor education. Incorporating mindful and meditative practices into an outdoor learning program can help improve mental and physical outcomes for children and educators.

A Prescription for Nature

Twenty years after the rise of shinrin-yoku in Japan, researchers in the United States were noticing those same examples of depression and high stress levels, but this time in children. In 2005, Richard Louv published the groundbreaking book Last Child in the Woods: Saving Our Children From Nature-Deficit Disorder. The book describes an epidemic of illness (both physical and mental) among youth who had become disconnected from the natural world. Louv outlines paths to countering nature-deficit disorder, ranging from more access to wild space to changing norms related to risk and messiness. One major policy change he explores is adding outdoor curriculum to schools and improving outdoor spaces. Since its publication in 2005, Last Child in the Woods has helped fuel a movement away from electronic and indoor play and toward reconnecting with the natural world.

The prescription of Last Child in the Woods is similar to that of shinrin-yoku: we need more exposure to nature. The idea that simply being in an environment can have positive effects is both simple and groundbreaking. In this mainstream,

[1] What Does the Research Say?, 2023

[2] Stressed? Take a 20 minute "nature pill", 2019

digitally-connected culture, we have lost our basic connection to the natural world around us. Children can name more apps than constellations and more superheroes than native plants. It is time we acknowledge that as human beings we are deeply connected to nature–to the forests, mountains, and water. If we deprive ourselves and our children of these interactions, we cannot be truly whole.

Indigenous Wisdom

If we were more in tune within our natural world as a society, there would be no need to conceptualize SEL and ecotherapy practices. In Indigenous cultures across the world, all rhythms and aspects of the natural world are interwoven within the fibers of daily life. Indigenous pathways of being include the transmission of values and culture through Earth-wisdom. There is gratitude and reverence toward natural elements and rites of passage.

Decolonizing pedagogical practices is crucial on the journey of experiencing ourselves as interconnected with the natural world. A great first step is researching the land in your area to learn more about its living cultures and history. The Native Land Digital Platform provides a mapping system for visitors to discover more regarding the Indigenous territories, languages, and treaties within a particular area.

It is important to understand that Indigenous peoples, their lifeways, and their deep connection to the Earth are still present. We honor them by upholding the spirit of the natural world and encouraging a sense of interconnectedness as one Earth family.

© 2023 Partners for Education, Agriculture, and Sustainability

Social and Emotional Activities for Learning Outdoors

Take students to an outdoor space where they will be comfortable standing and moving around for 10-20 minutes. Review safety guidelines and boundaries with students before you begin. Lessons marked with a *rain or shine icon* can be conducted on days with inclement weather. In this section you will find the following activities:

Action Path	Greeting Our Garden	Quote of the Day in Chalk
Breathe in Nectar, Breathe Out Buzz	Let's Get Small	Read-Alouds Under a Tree
Compost Your Concerns	Mirroring Nature	Seed Dreams
Dancing Leaves	Natural Affirmations	Sensory Scavenger Hunt
Five Senses Centering	Nature Band	Weather Check
Five Senses Snacking	Notice a Single Sound	Weather the Storm
	One With Nature	

Action Path

SKILLS TARGETED:

- Personal responsibility
- Environment stewardship

Brainstorm with your class how they and other students can help care for their campus grounds and campus wildlife. Create a list of short ideas that students can write on the sidewalk outside of the school to inspire other students and families to care for and connect with the world around them. Invite students to draw images to grab attention and inspire actions. Some actionable ideas to get you started:

- Pick up 10 pieces of litter today.
- Hug your favorite tree.
- Turn off lights that are not being used.
- Walk or bike somewhere instead of driving.
- Turn off the faucet while brushing your teeth.

Breathe in Nectar, Breathe Out Buzz

SKILLS TARGETED:

- Self-regulation
- Calming
- Focus

Invite the students to create a circle with you. In this exercise, we will focus on our breathing.

Together, let's pretend we are bees. Let's bring our bee wings (arms) out to our sides. As we fly, we will slowly lift our wings and take a nice deep breath in through our noses, feeling the cool air as we fly through the sky. Then, breathe out, slowly lowering our wings, bringing our hands back down to our bee's knees. Let's do that two more times. Breathing in, we can smell the sweet nectar of a bright yellow flower, breathing out, "Buzzzz." We landed on the flower. Take one more big breath in, lifting our wings, and when we breathe out through our mouths, we will "Buzz" all together. We will take four buzzing breaths. We will breathe in through our noses, lifting our wings to fly in the sky, and then drop our wings down, buzzing our breath out of our mouths as we land on a bright beautiful yellow flower.

○ # Compost Your Concerns

SKILLS TARGETED:

- Self-expression
- Self-regulation

Have your students write down their negative feelings and concerns on a piece of paper or even a leaf (if enough are readily available). Rip them up and throw them into the compost. Have a discussion about how these stresses are now being broken down into tiny bits of soil! This activity can be as short as three minutes at the beginning or end of learning. When we acknowledge the feelings of our students, we provide a safe space for students to process and overcome insecurities and stressors.

Dancing Leaves

SKILLS TARGETED:

- Self-regulation
- Calming

Walk with the students around the garden space. Ask them to collect a leaf from the ground (remind them not to pick the growing leaves). Once each child has a leaf, let them find a comfortable place to sit in the garden. Model holding the leaf on your palm close to your face. Starting with slow, calm breaths, try to move the leaf without letting it fall off your hand. Slowly increase your breathing to make the leaf dance in your palm. If your leaf falls, simply place it back on your palm and start slowly breathing again. When we are calm, we can control our breathing and ourselves. How does the leaf feel when it dances in your hand? How do you feel when you are calm?

For an extension, when you have finished the breathing activity, pass out paper and crayons. Model how to make a leaf rubbing. Once rubbings are complete, students can add words or drawings that describe how they feel when they are calm.

Five Senses Centering

SKILLS TARGETED:

- Mindfulness
- Self-management

This is a common SEL practice that provides even more benefits when it is taken outdoors while being among natural elements. Teachers are encouraged to participate in the activity while leading. Count the items on your fingers.

Five things you can see:
Look for five different natural elements around you.

Four things you can feel:
Pay attention to your body and find four natural sensations you can feel. Perhaps you feel the wind through your hair, sun on your skin, feet on the mulch, or a rock you are holding.

Three things you can hear:
What three things can you hear in the natural world around you? Listen for birds tweeting, bugs buzzing, children playing, and more.

Two things you can smell:
If the space allows, let students move silently within the area to find two different scents. This can also be done from a seated position with whatever is closest. Air, grass, soil, and their own skin are likely scents they will be able to access.

One thing you can taste:
Imagine the taste of the rain, nectar, a fruit, or a vegetable.

Five Senses Snacking

SKILLS TARGETED:

- Mindfulness
- Mindful consumption

Snack on something from the garden. Make sure you wash the produce with the students before eating it, and make sure you know whether students have any related allergies.

Today we will be tasting some vegetables and fruits in our outdoor space. We will take our time and really enjoy this experience by focusing on our five senses while we taste our snacks.

- How does it look?
- How does it smell?
- Is there a sound it makes while you chew?
- If you are picking it up with your hands, what does it feel like?
- Before you take that first bite, who can you thank for that food? Example response: *The worms that nourished the soil, the sun for helping it grow, the rain for watering it, the gardener who tended it...*
- Chew that first bite really slowly. What do you notice about the texture?
- How does this taste compare to other vegetables and fruits in the garden?
- How does this snack compare to your favorite food?

Greeting Our Garden

SKILLS TARGETED:

- Empathy
- Environmental stewardship

When approaching your outdoor learning space, begin to take notice of any stones, trees, and other natural elements. Some greetings we could encourage are:

> "Open up your arms, give yourself a hug, say, 'I'm lovable!...' Yes, you are, just like the plants!"
>
> "Look, the tree is waving! Let's wave back! Hello, tree!"
>
> "Blow a kiss to the garden!"
>
> "What do you think this plant's name is?"

Our garden is a community of living things that includes us! Today we will be greeting our garden. All living things are connected. From the air we breathe to the way we treat one another, life surrounds us. Just as we like to be treated with kindness, so does our garden. In this part of the game, students will introduce their partner to something they like about the garden. Before the game begins, allow students 1-2 minutes to find and connect with one organism or feature in the garden. This is their "garden friend." Remind students that their garden friend can be living (ants, plants, spiders) or nonliving (soil, rocks, air, clouds, wind). If their garden friend is living, they should be gentle and not move it from its habitat.

Partners split up and find someone else to introduce themselves to and meet a garden friend with. Players go around trying to meet as many other players as possible in one to two minutes.

SKILLS TARGETED

- Mindfulness

Guided imagery is a mindfulness process that uses visualization and imagination to bring awareness to the mind-body connection.

Find a comfortable place in the garden, field, or classroom on a rainy day. Students may lie on their backs or sit in a relaxed position. Read the following guided visualization:

Imagine our outdoor space. Picture the plants and how they bend slowly in the breeze.

Think about the animals that live in our space…
the snail moving slowly across a leaf…
the bird perched quietly on a branch…

Maybe a roly-poly is just opening up its shell to greet the day. Our garden is a safe place where insects and birds, squirrels and lizards, can all exist in peace.

Now imagine that you are standing in our garden.
You are safe and calm in our garden.

As you continue to breathe in through your nose…
out through your mouth… you begin to shrink.

With every breath out, you get a little smaller.

This shrinking feels tingly and safe. Smaller and smaller with every breath until you are a tiny version of yourself.

Now the snail is almost as tall as you.
The roly-poly is now the size of a playful dog.
It is time to explore the garden as your tiny self.

Keep your eyes closed and wander our garden.
Look for a place where you feel happy and safe.
What do you see there? Are there other animals there with you?

How can you help make this garden space even more beautiful? Would you like to grow something? Anything you want you can plant in our magic garden.

You may even plant seeds of peace … and of joy and happiness … and of calmness … or any other qualities you would like to increase or bring in your life …

This is your own space … This is a very magical time.

© 2023 Partners for Education, Agriculture, and Sustainability

Mirroring Nature

SKILLS TARGETED:

- Collaboration
- Communication

Assign students a partner. Introduce that they will be mirroring each other's movements to practice communication and collaboration. Students face their partner and choose who will be the mirror, or the person reflecting the other's movements. The teacher provides a theme which students will act out, reminding students to make appropriate choices. Students start mirroring activity while the teacher walks and monitors activity. After a few minutes, students will switch roles with their partner, so that both students have the experience mirroring and being mirrored.

At close, the teacher gathers students to reflect upon their experience in the activity. Did they like being mirrored? How did it feel to not know what they were going to do next and to have to trust their partner? What was fun, and what was difficult about the mirroring activity?

Examples of outdoor-related themes for mirroring:

- Gardening tasks
- Plants growing
- Plant life cycle
- Animal life cycles
- Animals in the garden
- Changing seasons

Natural Affirmations

SKILLS TARGETED

- Positive thinking
- Confidence
- Self-love

Explain to students that we talk to ourselves in our mind all day without thinking about what we say. It is important that we intentionally make sure we are sending ourselves periodic positive messages to encourage ourselves. An example might be before we read a book aloud to our friends. If we are nervous to read aloud, we might say, "You've got this!"

Nature provides for all of our basic needs, and we can rely on nature for support. Prompt students to make similes that affirm the qualities they have in common with other elements of nature. Affirmations should be repeated frequently so they stay with us. Here are some examples:

Like a tree, I am strong yet flexible.

Like a rock, I can weather strong storms.

Like the water, I can get around
the obstacles in my path.

Invite students to share aloud or record their affirmations to revisit later when they need them most.

Nature Band

SKILLS TARGETED:

- Teamwork
- Imagination
- Self-expression

To begin, sit the group in a circle and begin making one nature or animal sound repetitively, creating a beat. The next person creates a new nature-based sound, following the beat. The next student adds their own nature-based sound, and the music gets more complex. Each person repeats their sound until everyone has joined the band. As an extension, the teacher or a student can be the conductor, and students make sounds when they are directed to by the conductor.

Post-game discussion may include:

- What was the sound you were making?
- How is that sound made in nature?
- How did you feel when you heard our song?

Notice a Single Sound

SKILLS TARGETED:

- Self-regulation
- Focus
- Spacial awareness
- Calming

Deer are quiet observers. They use their long, fuzzy ears to listen carefully. There is a diversity of sounds that students can hear outdoors. Have students choose a spot outside. Invite students to stand or sit and focus on a specific sound. Suggest to students that they close their eyes. Invite students to think about the below prompts:

- Describe the sound.
- How does the sound make you feel?
- What is a connection you have with the sound? Have you heard this sound before? Does this sound remind you of anything?
- Share your thoughts about the sound and any feelings about the sound.

One With Nature

SKILLS TARGETED:

- Calming
- Mindfulness

Students have the choice to sit, stand, or lie down (provide a tarp when outdoors). Students may close their eyes if they wish as the teacher guides the class through the following body scan meditation.

Head: We are nature, where all things need water to live. Invite students to begin lightly tapping fingertips on the top of their heads. Imagine the rain is drizzling on our heads. Gently move the tapping down to our foreheads and faces. The water flows over our faces. We are like happy flowers feeling the rain.

Heart: We are nature, full of energy. Invite students to place hands on their hearts, breathing in and out with the breeze. Notice how our bodies contract and expand, life flowing through all on its own.

Upper body: We are like trees, with branches for arms that sway in the wind and stretch toward the sun. Invite students to sway their arms or stretch in any way that feels comfortable to them. We can reach up, we can sway over and stretch to the left, then to the right. Our hands are like leaves, feeling the warmth of the sun. Like flowers that open and then close to rest.

Lower body: Our feet are like roots, deep in friendship with the Earth. Invite students to wiggle their toes and stretch their legs in any way that feels comfortable to them.

Close with a self-hug and offer thanks to the Earth by blowing kisses through the wind!

Quote of the Day in Chalk

SKILLS TARGETED:

- Social awareness
- Empathy
- Self-expression

Prepare ahead of time by writing a quote in chalk on a walkway.

Introduce a quote relevant to what your students are learning or to a shared experience—for example, a quote about taking care of the environment or the beauty of nature. Facilitate a whole-class discussion, group students into pairs, or have each student share a one-word response to the quote. Then, students record their reflections with chalk around the quote. Students may respond in words, drawings, or emojis. A multimedia response provides students the choice of how they would like to respond to the quote. Students can express if they agree or disagree with the quote and also their peers' responses (as long as all responses are respectful and appropriate). This activity also gives students insight into the perspectives and feelings of their peers.

Read-Alouds Under a Tree

SKILLS TARGETED:

- Environmental stewardship
- Collaboration
- Mindfulness

Choose an SEL or environmentally focused read-aloud. Read through the book with your class, stopping frequently to make social and emotional and ecological connections. Allow students to be a part of the discussion. Moving your read-aloud outdoors gives a new context to your readings, and simply sitting in the presence of a tree can have positive psychological benefits.

After reading aloud, the teacher reflects with students about the experience of reading outside.

- Did you enjoy reading outside? Why or why not?
- What went well reading outside? What could we work on next time?
- How is a read-aloud different outside than inside the classroom?

Seed Dreams

SKILLS TARGETED:

- Collaboration
- Imagination
- Self expression

Place future seeds that will be planted in a glass or plastic jar. Provide each student with paper (such as sticky notes) and pencils so they can write words of motivation or affirmation to surround the seeds. Then, when the seeds are in season they will be fully energized!

Writing prompts could include:

- I have a dream that each seed will...
- I am excited to plant you because...
- When you grow into a plant, I hope...

Sensory Scavenger Hunt

SKILLS TARGETED:

- Mindfulness
- Focus

Give students a list of 5-10 adjectives and identify an area for them to explore. Tell students that they should use their silent insect walking feet to go find the objects. After 10 minutes ask students to circle up to share their findings. Make sure to remind them to only pick things that are in abundance.

Enjoy this starter list of adjectives:

- Bumpy
- Rough
- Smooth
- Dry
- Flat
- Moist
- Patterned
- Bright
- Dull
- Fragrant

Weather Check

SKILLS TARGETED:

- Encouragement
- Listening skills
- Community building

Rainy days are sometimes compared to sad feelings. Sunny days are often compared to happy feelings. But just like the plants in our garden, people need both rainy and sunny feelings to be healthy. Today we will take turns representing and then naming an emotion. This can be how we are truly feeling or what we want to act out based on the current weather. The first person will act out an emotion, then the group asks together, "How do you feel?" The first person then says, for example: "Oh I feel...sad." Everyone in the circle is invited to make a heart shape with their hands, and say, "Whatever your weather, we're here for you!" The next person has a turn and so on. To close, the teacher invites students to embrace themselves in a hug!

Weather the Storm

SKILLS TARGETED:

- Self-regulation
- Listening skills
- Problem solving

Have students find a comfortable place to sit or stand outdoors.

Ask students to consider how trees weather strong winds, rains, and extreme temperatures outdoors. Invite students to sit or stand up straight, close their eyes, and breathe deeply. The teacher has students imagine roots growing below their feet or seats, with their torsos straight and strong like tree trunks. A storm comes with cold temperatures, strong winds, and heavy rains. The teacher encourages students to sway in the wind, possibly with outstretched arms, but to use the strength of their roots and trunks to weather the storm. Students take deep breaths to calm their bodies as they sway and notice their emotions. The teacher then invites students to take a deep breath together and blow away the storm. To close the activity, have students imagine they are pulling up their roots with a wiggle and softening their trunks to bodies once more with a couple of twists from side to side.

Outdoor Learning for All Abilities

Outdoor learning is for students of all abilities! Physical, emotional, and learning differences or challenges should not interfere with access to quality outdoor education. It is important to keep the inclusion of all your students in mind and to be well versed in their specific needs, individual education plans, and 504 Accommodations before heading outside. While the specific needs of your students may vary widely, there are some key considerations when planning outdoor activities that will benefit all learners.

What's the Big Idea?

It is easy to get lost in the minutia of lesson planning and lose sight of the big picture. When we think about accommodating all learners, it is helpful to focus on the big idea of your lesson and find a way to give each student access. What is the high value objective of your lesson? Can this objective be made tangible in a way that a student with hearing or vision loss can explore? Is there a way for a child with an intellectual disability to experience the subject joyfully? How can you reach the most meaningful version of your lesson for each learner? With the big idea as your starting point, it is possible to find ways to ensure everyone learns and grows together outside.

Sensory Approach

With your big idea in mind, consider the specific needs of your students. Some students may only be able to conduct limited academic tasks. Others may have mobility issues or communication challenges. In these cases, using a sensory approach may be a good option. How can you introduce your content using sensory inputs? Would a student like to hold the seeds being described in the lesson? Hear the sound of a rain stick while talking about weather? Smell the fresh mint during a lesson on herbs? Do they like physical interaction or being read to by peers? Or would they prefer a quiet place for sensory exploration? You know your students best and, with a little planning, can make your lessons of high value for all learners.

Co-Teaching and Collaboration

In the inclusion setting there may be another teacher or teaching assistant who joins your class to help out. Consider sharing your outdoor lessons with other inclusion teachers in advance. They may have insights and ideas to help make the experience more enriching. Everyone benefits within a neurally diverse classroom. All students gain the opportunity to show leadership, empathy, and love. Are there students in the class who would enjoy assisting a friend? Encourage your class to help everyone meet their learning potential.

Least Restrictive Environment

In many ways, outdoor learning can truly represent the least restrictive environment. Overstimulating sounds are more easily diminished or ignored outside. The overcrowding often found in the classroom can be reduced. Physical behaviors that might be distracting indoors can be less consequential. Most of all, there are endless opportunities for student autonomy and self-guidance. Allowing the outdoor space to engage the student, and giving them the freedom to explore it, is a powerful learning tool. With careful planning, and the needs of your students in mind, the outdoor learning space can be a positive and empowering environment for all learners.

Outdoor Accessibility

Is your outdoor space accessible to all students? Could a student using a wheelchair operate easily in your space? Are there obstacles or hazards that might interfere for a student living with hearing or vision loss? Are there ways technology can supplement the students' outdoor learning? Would a peer scribing model make sense? It is key to think through all the obstacles to outdoor accessibility before heading out the door. That said, be prepared to be flexible and to pivot when some solutions turn out less than ideal. As with any of your lessons, sometimes what looks good on paper doesn't always work out in real life. Go easy on yourself and make course corrections as needed. Learning is a lifelong endeavor for us all!

Nature Nuggets: Techniques for Creating Joyful Connections

The following are examples of techniques that PEAS educators use to create a deeper connection between the students and their outdoor environment. These Nature Nuggets also act as a channel for "distractions" one may encounter in urban and other outdoor natural spaces. They build flexibility and create a sense of curiosity and joyful connection.

Greeting Your Outdoor Space

At PEAS we like to establish transition routines for our students. These are a few practices that facilitate an easy transition into your outdoor lesson and uphold our mission of cultivating joyful connections to ourselves and the natural world.

If possible, the outdoor educator will gather students for direct instruction or small group activities in a circle shape. Circles are important shapes in nature and many cultures. The students and the outdoor educator will sit together in a circle to communicate within a collaborative, respectful, and positive learning environment. The outdoor educator sits with students in the circle to represent their role as a facilitator of learning and in direct and open communication.

A great way to transition into a new space is to do something that physically acknowledges the transition. When the outdoor educator greets the students, we invite students to greet themselves in this new space by hugging themselves and saying, "I'm lovable!" The educator replies, "Yes, you are, just like our garden."

We like to greet the natural elements in the outdoor space such as insects, flowers, trees, vegetables, and even favorite rocks! Saying hello to outdoor elements eliminates the nature/human binary and builds camaraderie with the nonliving and living beings in the outdoors. Students also speak and learn the names of plants, animals, and nonliving parts of the natural environment. When we encourage and speak about environmental interdependence between human and outdoor elements, students can understand themselves as Earthkeepers and recognize their role within nature.

Turning Distractions into Connections

Natural elements in the outdoor space may also be distracting for students. Saying thank you to living and nonliving parts of the space is a gentle acknowledgment of the students'

interest and the presence of these beings in the habitat. It also serves as a moment of gratitude and a relaxed redirection of the students' attention.

Let's say thanks to the roly-polies for the work they do to break down the organic matter in our soil and let them get back to their job...

© 2023 Partners for Education, Agriculture, and Sustainability

Be a Conduit, Not a "Can't-do-it"

Unexpected visitors to your outdoor lesson can also be an opportunity to practice mindfulness. A cardinal perched on a nearby tree can provide the students and teacher a chance to be silent and still in order to observe a peaceful moment of another being. When we practice this type of mindfulness, students internalize the attributes and behaviorism of living beings.

Often in urbanized environments we will encounter planes overhead that could cause a disruption, but instead we allow this to be another opportunity to ground ourselves. As a plane flies overhead, drowns out a teacher's voice, and the students inevitably look up, say "Let's take a plane break! Send the plane on its way through the sky!" Students and teachers take a deep collective breath and blow toward the plane.

Acknowledging Fears in the Garden

PEAS outdoor educators understand that our students are coming from a variety of backgrounds, and some may have experienced trauma in the outdoors or have family histories that have caused serious concerns with being outdoors. Our goal as outdoor educators is to meet students where they are in their relationship with the outdoors and encourage deeper connections to the world.

Additionally, when fears are caused by allergies or genuine phobias, we do our absolute best to remind the children to take as much space from bees, spiders, wasps, etc. as they need to feel safe. At PEAS we also seek to build or repair relationships with pollinators, arachnids, and other garden fauna. In a garden habitat, spiders and pollinators have valuable roles in the ecosystem. We encourage a respect and understanding of their importance and behaviors. In a healthy garden, these living beings are less prone to aggressive behaviors, as all their needs are met. We invite students to "look with their eyes," observing with space and careful, gentle movements the beautiful dance of pollination and intricate webmaking. With that being said, we also educate our students on common venomous spiders, locations of fire ants and wasp nests, and protective measures for respecting the homes of these garden companions.

Deepening Connection with the Natural World

In tandem with hands-on activities, PEAS educators use these nature nuggets to deepen connection to the natural world. We have found that providing consistent routines and following these practices creates a sense of community and kinship that students internalize. We are consistently seeing their attitudes toward their environment become more positive and enthusiastic.

The reciprocal relationship between humans and plant life is honored throughout Indigenous cultures and communities. We bring these symbiotic rituals into our gardening practices at PEAS because we believe them to be foundational for young people to build empathy, generosity, and kindness.

Hug the trees: From a very young age, children understand that trees provide us with the oxygen we breathe. This is a positive foundation for building the relationships between humans and trees. The outdoor educator often invites children to embrace various trees in their outdoor environments. We hope to inspire children to create and sustain bonds with trees, animals, and other natural elements they will encounter throughout their lives. We believe that there is a sense of kinship that children feel organically with the natural world. We celebrate and honor these connections by providing opportunities for children to take pride in their admiration for their Earth family.

Seed wishes: The outdoor educator gathers students in a circle. Before the outdoor educator passes out seeds, they invite students to receive the seed, hug them in their hand (closed palm), and even hold them up to the sun. Students will hold their closed palm to their heart and think a happy thought for the seed. For example, "I hope you grow big and strong," or simply "Thank you, seed." When covering seeds with their blanket of soil, we say "Sweet dreams, little seed!"

Planting transplants: The outdoor educator gathers students in a circle to greet the transplant. "Hello, tomato!" The outdoor educator models how to remove the transplant from the pot. Students pass around the transplant and say kind, encouraging words. This is a great practice if there are not enough individual transplants for each student to plant. The outdoor educator can show the roots system, give a gentle hug to remove from the container, and "tickle the roots" of the transplant to encourage root growth.

NOTE:

Specific transplant and seed planting methods in a garden or outdoor space are a case-by-case practice. Check with your administration and collaborate with your faculty about where and what to plant. There is no wrong or right way to bring the experience of "seed wishes" to students, however many schools have pre-established plans and methods for their gardens.

Harmonious harvesting: Before harvesting, the outdoor educator considers influential factors of the plants such as stage of life, season, abundance, and timing. Is the plant going to seed, and soon will no longer fruit? Is there an impending freeze or heat wave which will impact future harvests? Is the plant bearing enough produce for a sustainable harvest? Is your school community closing for any holidays or breaks which will impede future harvests? Do other entities such as PTA, garden to cafeteria, or fellow teachers have plans for the produce? These are a few criteria to keep in mind before harvesting.

A pillar of Indigenous harvesting is to honor the plants and trees. The outdoor educator invites students to gather around plants. Together students and teachers give reverence to plants with words or gentle touch, saying words of gratitude for sharing the fruit they work so hard to produce. Students then harvest a specified amount from the plant, and as an action of reciprocity, can complete some of the below tasks as gifts:

- Offering water
- Enriching the soil with fresh compost
- Sowing nitrogen-rich seeds, such as black-eyed peas
- Planting mushroom blocks
- Filling ollas

Closing Reflections

During the conclusions of our time with our students, we take time to recognize and celebrate their dedication and positive impact on the outdoor environment. The outdoor educator invites students to hug themselves, say goodbye to the space or a special natural element of their choice. "Blow a kiss to the farm/garden/park. Say goodbye to your favorite tree!" For more reflection routines and ideas, see our section Fun and Easy PEASy Reflections.

Creating Your Outdoor PEAce Area

With districts across the nation incorporating social and emotional learning and restorative practices into their programs and initiatives, many educators have become familiar with the benefits of creating a peace area or reflection zone in the classroom. Students spend long hours at school and are expected to be on their best behavior throughout the day. Asking a child to remain regulated and in control for this long is unrealistic. All children need to know it is okay to make mistakes and not handle every situation with grace. They should be confident they can take a break when they feel the need to regroup. We are all worthy of love and belonging. Some students, for a variety of reasons, have greater difficulty self-regulating and/or focusing.

A peace area is a great spot for students who are overstimulated or just need additional time to process a situation or regain composure to take a moment to figure out what they need. Students are actively learning how to regulate their emotions. We cannot punish them under the assumption they are already experts in this skill. Truthfully, this learning continues throughout our adult lives, and students are just taking their first steps on this journey.

A peace area can provide both physical and psychological tools to support students as they process their emotions. An outdoor PEAce area needs to be portable, so we suggest finding a lunch box or toolkit that can be converted into a "to-go" PEAce Box. This may be a smaller version of your indoor peace corner and provide familiar prompts and objects for assisting with calming or may be made to incorporate items from the natural world. Once outdoors, find an appropriate space to set up your PEAce area. Students in the PEAce Zone should have enough space from the whole group to self-regulate, but also be able to observe the activities of their classmates. An intentional proximity to the class will encourage a student to reintegrate into class activities with more confidence.

Below are some of our suggestions, but this is a great opportunity for you to collaborate with your students and come up with something that is meaningful to them.

If you notice a child having a hard time self-regulating, invite them to spend a few minutes in the PEAce area. The PEAce area should never be seen as a punishment. Students should know that they are welcome to rejoin the class as soon as they feel ready. You can recommend to the student that they choose two to three activities so they can feel better in their bodies, hearts, and minds. Each child will need a different amount of time, depending on their situation. If the child does not rejoin the class on their own, invite them back after 5-10 minutes. Some situations may require longer time to regain calm.

Additionally, students might also ask to have time with the PEAce box or in the PEAce area. Many students who are outwardly showing no signs of dysregulation can benefit from taking a break and having a moment of calm.

Items to consider having in your PEAce Box:

A list of physical calming techniques that students already know and have practiced, such as:

— Balloon breathing
— Body scan
— Draw a picture of your feelings
— Stretch your body
— Shake it off
— Close your eyes and count backwards 10-1
— Tapping
— Write a letter to your teacher or a friend
— Seed sorting
— Whisper singing

Natural items that are interesting to observe:
Provide a magnifying glass so students can look at these items up close. The process of focusing deeply will automatically help calm a body.

— Bird feathers
— Pine or magnolia cones
— Various types of seeds or seed pods
— A real sponge
— Ball moss
— Various leaves
— Shells
— Any other items of interest that promote curiosity

Other items:

— Fidget gadgets for those who need them
— Paper on a clipboard
— Pens, pencils, markers, and/or crayons
— Books

Having a few related to the lesson topic allows for students to stay engaged while giving them a little space from the group. Having books related to processing emotions can help with self-regulation.

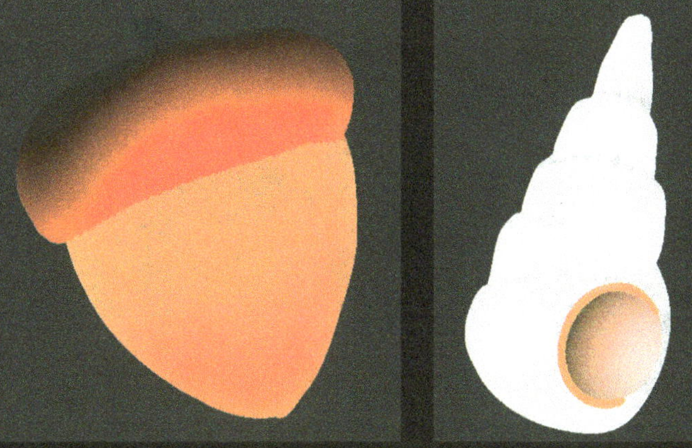

Having a functioning PEAce Area as part of your outdoor classroom is one more way to ensure successful outcomes for all of your students. You may find in time that your students begin to self-regulate and find their own calming techniques in the garden. Until then, it is a good idea to have a plan in place for how and where students can find some peace. A PEAce Area is a great way to introduce strategies for managing emotions, and we can all benefit from having these systems in place.

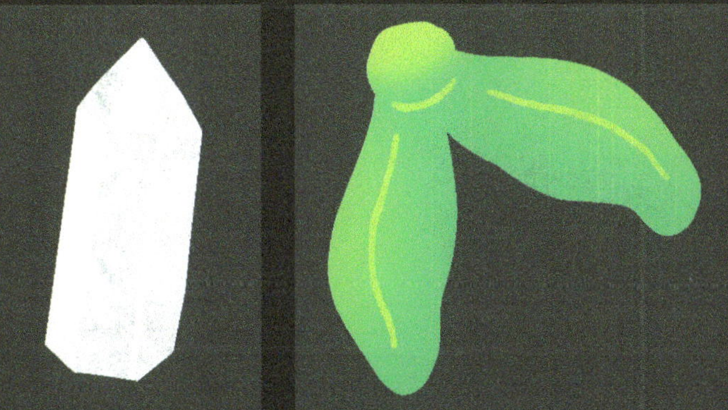

© 2023 Partners for Education, Agriculture, and Sustainability

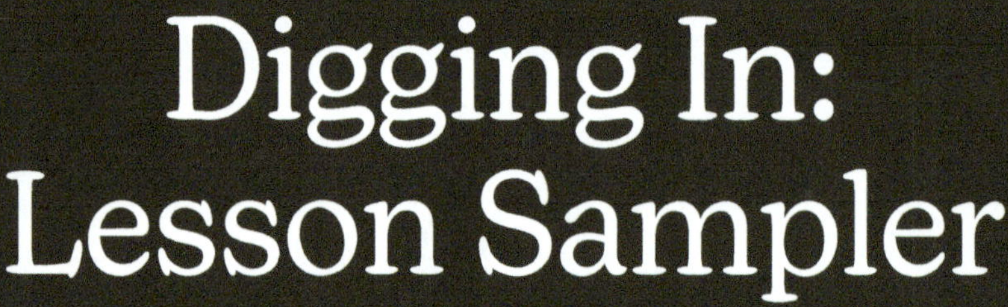

PART III

Digging In:
Lesson Sampler

PEAS' Engaging Lessons for Outdoor Learning

The following section of the guidebook will include ready-to-go PEAS outdoor lessons in a variety of subject areas that you can use with your class. These lessons have been created with ease of use in mind and are designed to keep materials and prep to a minimum. Each lesson should be viewed as a guide, so feel free to let your own creativity augment and enhance them for your class's particular needs.

Each lesson includes specific alignment information for **TEKS** (Texas Essential Knowledge and Skills), **Common Core**, and **NGSS** (Next Generation Science Standards). You will also find **Special Education** and **English Language Learner** (ELL) accommodations following each lesson.

As you gain confidence teaching outside, you will inevitably want to design your own outdoor lessons. Below are some key considerations and questions to keep in mind as you begin to plan for the outdoors. Feel free to use this framework to help organize your thoughts and give structure to your plans.

Core Routines — Getting to the Lesson

Establishing core routines helps students transition from the classroom to outdoor learning space with ease. Just like other routines, they may take a little while to establish.

Facilitate transition to the garden: Give students clear directions for how they should enter the space, where they should sit or stand, and let them know how long it will be before you will go explore. Share how you will get the students' attention and practice it! Examples:

WORD OF THE DAY
For call and response

"When I say, water, you say cycle! Water...Cycle, Water... Cycle." Adding hand motions can help with vocabulary recall and enhance kinesthetic learning. "After we repeat this twice, I want all eyes on me and volume at level zero, so you can hear the next direction."

ANIMAL SOUNDS

"When you hear me crow like a rooster, stop, look, and listen for your next set of instructions.'

Create a Big Question: What do we want to learn about or explore today? This will set the tone and create focus for the students. In most public education settings, the teacher/facilitator will pick a question in advance to focus the lesson on the planned theme. In more flexible settings, it is extremely valuable to allow students to come up with their own questions to focus their learning. Sentence stems can be provided to help students articulate their thoughts.

Set expectations/boundaries for the day/activity. New boundaries for varying activities will need to be given throughout the lesson.

If there is a need for the partner-teacher or class volunteer to do something specific, let them know at the beginning of the lesson.

SET THE STAGE

Prepare students for what is ahead and/or generate excitement and curiosity about the topic. Use this time to activate prior knowledge.

Is there a **Big Idea** you hope the students walk away from the lesson with? A big idea can help center your lesson around one key piece of information.

Ask open-ended inquiry questions to come back to at the end of the lesson. Questions that start with how and why will elicit the connection to prior knowledge. Do you have a **Big Question** you would like them to consider throughout the lesson?

Examples of activities that set the stage:

- Have students make observations about the outdoor environment surrounding them
- Storytelling or a book: ask questions to hook their curiosity
- Short game
- Songs (call and response): great for introducing vocabulary and processes
- Graphics/artifacts:
  - *What do you notice about...?*
  - *Who can tell me what they see here?*

Teacher self-check for setting the stage:

- Do the kids actually participate in the opening?
- Are we activating prior knowledge?
- Are we letting the students do the thinking by asking open-ended questions?
- Is it short and sweet and actually engaging?

BREAKOUT PROCEDURE

In order to minimize "sit and get" time in an outdoor lesson, explanations should be sprinkled throughout the exploration. An anchor chart or visual aid shared briefly at the beginning of Set the Stage provides great support for all students, especially our language learners and students with hearing loss. Depending on the theme, this chart may be used for reference throughout the exploration.

- While students are exploring, you may want to stop the whole group for a one-minute circle to share a discovery.
- You may ask one group to go share an interesting discovery or fact with the other groups or you may want to share the information yourself.
- Continue to ask students questions throughout to prompt the next level of understanding.
  - *Yes or no questions will not give students the opportunity to make bigger connections.*
  - *How or why questions create open-ended questions that allow students to do the thinking.*
  - *Find out, "What do you* think?*"*

Teacher self-check for breakout procedure:

- Did students receive clear and concise information to guide their exploration?
- Did we create relevant conversations about the topic?

EXPLORE

To ensure the lesson is interactive and engaging, students should be allowed to explore for at least 60% of the lesson.

Explorations can take place independently or with their peers for at least 27 minutes of a 45-minute lesson or 36 minutes of a 60-minute lesson. The longer the better!

Facilitators/teachers connect vocabulary and concepts throughout exploration with small groups and individual students.

- Classroom teachers bridge connections between outdoors and the classroom.
- Facilitators ask questions to engage curiosity and promote conversation among the kids

On campuses where there is ample space, 27 minutes should allow time for students to explore two to three areas of an outdoor learning environment.

Do we need to record or synthesize our thinking? If so, what options will engage the students? Students should be given a choice and freedom to explore and to connect what they are learning through varied learning modalities (drawing, writing, painting, sculpture, creating a song or dance, etc...).

It is okay if we are just creating more questions!

Teacher self-check for exploration:

- Do we have the objectives in mind? Is our big question being explored?

- Are the students *doing?* Discovering? Learning? Inquiring? Observing? Touching? Sensing?

REFLECT & WRAP UP

Coming together at the end of class will reinforce lesson content, generate questions, and conclude the lesson. This is an opportunity to refer back to the anchor chart or other visuals.

- Come back to the inquiry question.

- Have students reflect on this again at the end of the class.

- Circle up and choose a reflection from Five Fun and Easy PEASy Reflections to see what:
  — *Students learned today?*
  — *Students connected with?*
  — *New questions came up?*

- Share information necessary to help them tie up loose ends in their understanding and encourage them to extend their learning at home.

- Revisit your **Big Idea** and **Big Question** from the beginning of the lesson. Check for understanding.

Teacher self-check for reflection and wrap-up:

- How do we know that students increased their understanding?

- Did the students leave asking relevant questions or talking about relevant events?

- Did written work, drawings, paintings, designs, and models reflect an understanding of content?

- Can students share relevant information with their peers?

EXTEND
After class or at home

This allows students to take learning further and/or to continue the learning in another setting or at a later time.

- When appropriate, give students a task or an action to apply outside of class or at home.

- Is there something they can explore in their home or community and bring back their findings next time?

- How can we connect new concepts (Big Ideas) to their world again in the future?

Transition to leave space:

- While students are still focused, share expectations for transitioning to the next lesson or activity.

© 2023 Partners for Education, Agriculture, and Sustainability

Other post-lesson teacher reflection questions for consideration:

- Did the kids move/interact for the majority of the lesson?

- Did the kids get their hands dirty?

- Did we promote healthy risk taking?

- Did we spend a majority (60%) of the time exploring something in the outdoor learning environment?

- Did kids talk more than the teacher talked?

- Did the majority of students engage, express curiosity, create new questions, or learn something new?

Community Wisdom

For items in blue, scan the code or visit
tinyurl.com/EZPZ-SocialStudies-1

OBJECTIVES

- Students understand that ecosystems include communities of diverse living beings, each with a valuable role.

- Students explore ways humans are related to other animals within the natural world.

- Students build upon a sense of camaraderie while cultivating classroom culture.

MATERIALS

— Clipboards to secure cards outdoors

— Index cards

— Pencils

— Crayons, markers, and/or colored pencils

— Clothespins

— Visual Aid of an Ecosystem Community

— Visual Aid of "Wise Grand Owl" Nature Name Tag

1 Set the Stage

- Show a visual aid of an example of an ecosystem consisting of food, water, shelter, and space with a community of producers, consumers, and decomposers.

- Begin with the **Big Question:**
"Are humans a part of nature? How are humans like other animals?"

- Present the **Big Idea:** "An ecosystem is like a community or a town, where many living beings and nonliving things have relationships with one another. These relationships help them to learn, grow, and survive in the wild."

- Discuss how living beings need sunlight and air to survive and grow healthy. All living beings require food, water, shelter, and space within an ecosystem.

- Discuss how the natural world requires many kinds of living beings and nonliving elements in order for the community to thrive and be strong. For example, if we didn't have plants or honeybees, the other consumers would go hungry. If we had no trees at all, it would be hard for us to breathe. All parts of the natural world are important to one another and come together to create a balanced ecosystem.

2 Breakout Procedure

- "When I say Who-Who, you say, You-You and show me your owl eyes." Use hands to make owl eyes. "Thank you, all eyes should now be on Wise Grand Owl."

- Explain that today we will become new animals living in an ecosystem community.

- Show students the "Wise Grand Owl" Nature Name Tag as a reference, "Notice how I wrote my nature name and I drew a picture."

- Invite students to imagine their own drawing and Nature Name: First, Middle, and Last (this ensures a variety of names even if there are several of the same favorite animal).

- Pass out clipboards with attached index cards.

- Pass out various writing utensils and remind students to kindly share.

- Welcome collaboration and problem-solving among the students.

3 Explore

- Students who finish early are invited to pin their Nature Name Tag to their clothes, water the garden, or explore the outdoor space as their nature-being character. Let them know you will call for them to rejoin the group once everyone has had time to finish their Nature Name Tag.

- Call all students back to your circle or group, and invite them to turn and talk with a classmate to discuss their nature-beings' strengths and skills. Give them the example, "I am Wise Grand Owl, and my strength is using my big owl eyes to see the greatness of everyone in our Earth family!"

- When you notice most students have completed and had time to discuss, call for their attention.

- "Who-who, You-You!" "Thank you! All eyes should now be on Wise Grand Owl."

- Gather the students to sit in a circle, "This is our Earth family, our community! I am so excited to meet everyone who is a part of our ecosystem. We will go around the circle and share our Nature Names and a skill or strength we bring to the community!"

- If there is time, let students act as their nature-beings to go and meet the other nature beings (students, plants, and elements) in the garden. Model how they can introduce themselves and talk to the other beings. While this may seem like a whimsical activity, it is a great way for students to start getting to know each other and their garden.

4 Reflect & Wrap-Up

- Ask: "How do all of our different strengths and skills help our ecosystem community?"

- "How can we help everyone in our Earth family feel respected?"

- "How can we work together as a community to take care of this outdoor space?"

5 Extension

- Create an ecosystem community "Wonder Wall" for pinning nature names and wonderings.

- Collaborate to choose or accentuate your designated outdoor learning space.

- Create Outdoor Learning Journals devoted to personal narratives students write from the perspectives of their nature-beings.

- Offer the opportunity to have a tradition of wearing Nature Name Tags during future outdoor lessons and for students to be called by their Nature Names.

- Invite students to collaborate to create ecosystem community guidelines.

- Create an Earth family song or cheer.

Social Studies TEKS

K.10 Culture — The student understands similarities and differences among individuals. The student is expected to identify similarities and differences among individuals such as kinship and religion.

1.14A — Describe and explain the importance of beliefs, language, and traditions of families and communities.

2.12A — Identify the significance of various ethnic and/or cultural celebrations.

3.10A — Explain the significance of various ethnic and/or cultural celebrations in the local community and other communities.

3.12 Culture — The student understands the importance of writers and artists to the cultural heritage of communities. The student is expected to identify how various writers and artists such as Kadir Nelson, Tomie dePaola, Carmen Lomas Garza, and Laura Ingalls Wilder and their stories, poems, statues, and paintings contribute to the cultural heritage of communities.

4.1B — Identify and compare the ways of life of American Indian groups in Texas before European exploration such as the Lipan Apache, Karankawa, Caddo, and Jumano.

4.1C — Describe the cultural regions in which American Indians lived such as Gulf, Plains, Puebloan, and Southeastern.

5.20B — Explain how examples of art, music, and literature reflect the times during which they were created.

5.21A — Describe customs and traditions of various racial, ethnic, and religious groups in the United States.

ELL Accommodations

Sentence stems
Peer turn and talk
Think, pair, share
Extra time for responses
Rephrase, repeat, or slow down
Pre-teach vocabulary
Visuals and verbal cues to reinforce spoken and written language
Graphic organizers
Hands-on activities
Non-verbal responses
Group work

SPED Accommodations

Sentence stems
Assistance with writing nature name tags
Moderate noise for sound sensitivity
Additional time for completion
Breaks/PEAS area
Rephrase, repeat, or slow down
Drawing or model representation
Visuals and verbal cues
Visual schedule
Pre-teach vocabulary

© 2023 Partners for Education, Agriculture, and Sustainability

Fawns Go Foraging

For items in blue, scan the code or visit
tinyurl.com/EZPZ-SocialStudies-2

OBJECTIVES

- Students explore the benefits of intentional listening in a natural environment.

- Students understand that there are societies and adaptive behaviors among animal groups.

- Students understand that humans acquire knowledge and skills by observing other animal patterns.

- Students experiment with their own sense of hearing in varying degrees.

- Students describe the sounds that exist in their outdoor learning area.

MATERIALS

- Poster representation of boundaries of your outdoor space
- Clipboards
- Pencils
- Colored pencils
- Visuals of deer
- Fawn's Exploration Guide

1 Set the Stage

- Display a poster with a simple map of your outdoor learning space.

- Begin with the **Big Question:** "What are some examples of nature sounds we might hear?"

- Present the **Big Idea:** "Listening and observing helps animals to learn and make decisions. For example, White-tailed Deer have incredible hearing and sight. Does, or mother deer, will often leave their offspring in a hiding place for several hours at a time to forage. When fawns reach maturity they will learn to forage with their mothers. Why might fawns need to learn early in life to listen closely for danger? Young deer will camouflage and hide. When mature they will swish their tails to warn their herd of a predator, often before ever being detected as prey."

- Introduce the concept of "Deer Ears": cupping in front/behind ears to amplify sound.

- Discuss how deer move quietly and listen closely in order to survive in the wild. They rotate their satellite-dish-like ears up to 180° to locate sound. Many adaptations allow deer to protect their herds and find the best habitats for raising young and foraging.

2 Breakout Procedure

- Introduce the Fawn's Exploration Guide. The fawn represents the student surrounded by the outdoors.

- Invite students to experiment with "Deer Ears" practice while exploring the sounds of nature, imagining they are a herd of deer foraging outdoors.

- Demonstrate using the Fawn's Exploration Guide that students will record the observations they hear in their outdoor learning environment. Drawings, symbols, lists, and labeling are all welcome ways to communicate their observations on paper.

- Students are also invited to include what they see on their Fawn's Exploration Guide.
- Review the outdoor boundaries for "fawn" (student) safety.

3 Explore

- Distribute the Fawn's Exploration Guide, clipboards, and pencils.
- Invite students to calmly and quietly explore the sights and sounds of their surroundings.
- Remind students to experiment with "Deer Ears" practice.
- While exploring, prompt with the following questions:
- "What sound was furthest from you? What sound was closest to you?"
- "What was the loudest sound that you heard? What was the quietest sound that you heard?"
- "What was the strangest sound you've heard so far?"

4 Reflect & Wrap-Up

- Call students back together. Challenge them to prance back to you like frolicking fawns! Countdown from 5-4-3-2-1, all eyes and ears on you.
- Ask: "How can we use deer wisdom in our everyday lives?"
- "What spot had the most food for foraging?"
- "What spot is the safest for fawns to hide?"
- "What did you learn about how deer thrive in the wild?"

5 Extension

- Deer naturally have a vast home range, estimated to one square mile. This home range is selected by the herd's prominent female. There is an opportunity to extend this lesson into exploring other potential outdoor learning spaces. We may ask: "How do animals decide where they will live and migrate? What different ways do animals cooperate?"

Social Studies TEKS

K.3A — Use spatial terms, including over, under, near, far, left, and right, to describe relative location.

K.4B — Identify how geographic location influences human characteristics of place such as shelter, clothing, food, and activities.

1.3A — Describe the location of self and objects relative to other locations in the classroom and school using spatial terms.

1.5B — Identify and describe how geographic location influences the human characteristics of place such as shelter, clothing, food, and activities.

2.16F — Create written and visual material such as stories, maps, and graphic organizers to express ideas.

3.3B — Identify and compare how people in different communities adapt to or modify the physical environment in which they live such as deserts, mountains, wetlands, and plains.

3.16E — Create written and visual material such as stories, pictures, maps, and graphic organizers to express ideas.

4.1B — Identify and compare the ways of life of American Indian groups in Texas before European exploration such as the Lipan Apache, Karankawa, Caddo, and Jumano.

4.7A — Explain the geographic factors such as landforms and climate that influence patterns of settlement and the distribution of population in Texas, past and present.

4.9A — Explain the economic activities various early American Indian groups in Texas used to meet their needs and wants such as farming, trading, and hunting.

5.8A — Describe how and why people have adapted to and modified their environment in the United States such as the use of human resources to meet basic needs.

ELL Accommodations

Sentence stems
Peer turn and talk
Think, pair, share
Extra time for responses
Gestures for new vocabulary
Rephrase, repeat, or slow down
Drawing or model representation
Visuals and verbal cues to reinforce spoken and written language
Hands-on activities
Non-verbal responses

SPED Accommodations

Sentence stems
Assistance with drawings, symbols, lists, and/or labeling
Moderate noise for sound sensitivity
Additional time for completion
Breaks/PEAS area
Rephrase, repeat, or slow down
Drawing or model representation
Visuals and verbal cues
Visual schedule
Pre-teach vocabulary
Rephrase, repeat, or slow down
Drawing or model representation
Visuals and verbal cues
Visual schedule
Pre-teach vocabulary

© 2023 Partners for Education, Agriculture, and Sustainability

Twenty-Twenty

OBJECTIVE

- Students practice adding and subtracting numbers that equal twenty.

MATERIALS

- Egg cartons: 1 per group of 2–3 students
- Small chalkboard or whiteboard and chalk or marker

1 Set the Stage

- Begin with the **Big Idea:** "There are many ways to add numbers together to equal 20."

- Present the **Big Question:** "What are some strategies for finding out which numbers will equal 20 when combined?"

- Say to students, "To sharpen our skills in math, we need to practice making and breaking a number quickly and correctly. Today we are going to go on a little hunt for the number 20."

- "I am going to give each group an egg carton [show carton] to organize your collection. How many cups are in a carton? [Answer: 12] We are going to be looking at these as pairs of cups. How many are in a pair? [Answer: 2] How many pairs of cups do we have in an egg carton? [Answer: 6]" Model by showing the 6 pairs.

- "The goal of our game is to collect 6 sets of the same objects in pairs of cups and make sure they add up to 20 in total. For example, I have 6 leaves in this cup, so how many leaves will I need to put in the other cup so I have 20 in total? [Answer: 14] We will check our work when we come back together."

- Establish a rule for collecting, "Only collect things that there are plenty of."

- Have students give examples: veggies, pebbles, leaves, mulch pieces, beans, flower petals (only if there are a whole bunch), etc.

2 Breakout Procedure

- "You will have 15 minutes to complete this collection."

- "When you hear me make this [insert animal] sound, meet me back here and we will check our collections together."

- Before sending students off to explore, let them know who they will be working with.

3 Explore

- Give students 15 minutes to collect items.

- Spot-check groups to make sure their items are adding to 20. Prompt students who need support.

- Bring students back together. Have students switch egg cartons with another group so they can check each other's work.

- Have students share out the number combos that add to twenty while the teacher records the numbers (using addition equations) on the whiteboard. If you have enough time, record all combinations. If short on time, try to get at least six combinations.

4   Reflect & Wrap-Up

- Think-pair-share: "When might we need to be able to add numbers quickly?"
- Group share: Pick a few students to share their partners' ideas.

Math TEKS

KINDER

K.1B — use a problem-solving model that incorporates analyzing given information, formulating a plan or strategy, determining a solution, justifying the solution, and evaluating the problem-solving process and the reasonableness of the solution.

K.1C — select tools, including real objects, manipulatives, paper and pencil, and technology as appropriate, and techniques, including;

K.1E — create and use representations to organize, record, and communicate mathematical ideas.

K.1F — analyze mathematical relationships to connect and communicate mathematical ideas.

K.2B — read, write, and represent whole numbers from 0 to at least 20 with and without objects or pictures.

K.2C — count a set of objects up to at least 20 and demonstrate that the last number said tells the number of objects in the set regardless of their arrangement or order;

K.2D — recognize instantly the quantity of a small group of objects in organized and random arrangements.

K.2E — generate a set using concrete and pictorial models that represents a number that is more than, less than, and equal to a given number up to 20;

K.2G — compare sets of objects up to at least 20 in each set using comparative language;

K.2I — compose and decompose numbers up to 10 with objects and pictures.

K.3A — model the action of joining to represent addition and the action of separating to represent subtraction;

K.3C — explain the strategies used to solve problems involving adding and subtracting within 10 using spoken words, concrete and pictorial models, and number sentences.

1ST GRADE

1.2C — select tools, including real objects, manipulatives, paper and pencil, and technology as appropriate, and techniques, including mental math, estimation, and number sense as appropriate, to solve problems; revised August 2022 8

1.1E — create and use representations to organize, record, and communicate mathematical ideas;

1.1F — analyze mathematical relationships to connect and communicate mathematical ideas; and

1.1G — display, explain, and justify mathematical ideas and arguments using precise mathematical language in written or oral communication.

1.2A — recognize instantly the quantity of structured arrangements;

1.2B — use concrete and pictorial models to compose and decompose numbers up to 120 in more than one way as so many hundreds, so many tens, and so many ones;

1.2C — use objects, pictures, and expanded and standard forms to represent numbers up to 120; 1.2D generate a number that is greater than or less than a given whole number up to 120;

1.2E — use place value to compare whole numbers up to 120 using comparative language;

© 2023 Partners for Education, Agriculture, and Sustainability

1.3A — use concrete and pictorial models to determine the sum of a multiple of 10 and a one-digit number in problems up to 99;

1.3B — use objects and pictorial models to solve word problems involving joining, separating, and comparing sets within 20 and unknowns as any one of the terms in the problem such as:
2 + 4 = [ ]; 3 + [ ] = 7; and 5 = [ ] - 3;

1.3C — compose 10 with two or more addends with and without concrete objects;

1.3D — apply basic fact strategies to add and subtract within 20, including making 10 and decomposing a number leading to a 10;

1.3E — explain strategies used to solve addition and subtraction problems up to 20 using spoken words, objects, pictorial models, and number sentences;

2.1C — select tools, including real objects, manipulatives, paper and pencil, and technology as appropriate, and techniques, including mental math, estimation, and number sense as appropriate, to solve problems;

2.1D — communicate mathematical ideas, reasoning, and their implications using multiple representations, including symbols, diagrams, graphs, and language as appropriate;

2.1E — create and use representations to organize, record, and communicate mathematical ideas;

2.1F — analyze mathematical relationships to connect and communicate mathematical ideas; and

2.1G — display, explain, and justify mathematical ideas and arguments using precise mathematical language in written or oral communication.

2.4A — recall basic facts to add and subtract within 20 with automaticity;

3.1C — select tools, including real objects, manipulatives, paper and pencil, and technology as appropriate, and techniques, including mental math, estimation, and number sense as appropriate, to solve problems;

3.1D — communicate mathematical ideas, reasoning, and their implications using multiple representations, including symbols, diagrams, graphs, and language as appropriate;

3.2E — create and use representations to organize, record, and communicate mathematical ideas;

3.3F — analyze mathematical relationships to connect and communicate mathematical ideas; and

3.4G — display, explain, and justify mathematical ideas and arguments using precise mathematical language in written or oral communication

4.1C — select tools, including real objects, manipulatives, paper and pencil, and technology as appropriate, and techniques, including mental math, estimation, and number sense as appropriate, to solve problems;

4.1D — communicate mathematical ideas, reasoning, and their implications using multiple representations, including symbols, diagrams, graphs, and language as appropriate;

4.1E — create and use representations to organize, record, and communicate mathematical ideas;

4.1F — analyze mathematical relationships to connect and communicate mathematical ideas; and

4.1G — display, explain, and justify mathematical ideas and arguments using precise mathematical language in written or oral communication.

5.1C — select tools, including real objects, manipulatives, paper and pencil, and technology as appropriate, and techniques, including mental math, estimation, and number sense as appropriate, to solve problems;

5.1D — communicate mathematical ideas, reasoning, and their implications using multiple representations, including symbols, diagrams, graphs, and language as appropriate;

5.1E — create and use representations to organize, record, and communicate mathematical ideas;

5.1F — analyze mathematical relationships to connect and communicate mathematical ideas; and

5.1G — display, explain, and justify mathematical ideas and arguments using precise mathematical language in written or oral communication.

Common Core Standards

CCSS.MATH.CONTENT.K.CC.A.3 — Write numbers from 0 to 20. Represent a number of objects with a written numeral 0-20 (with 0 representing a count of no objects).

CCSS.MATH.CONTENT.K.CC.B.5 — Count to answer "how many?" questions about as many as 20 things arranged in a line, a rectangular array, or a circle, or as many as 10 things in a scattered configuration; given a number from 1-20, count out that many objects.

CCSS.MATH.CONTENT.K.OA.A.1 — Represent addition and subtraction with objects, fingers, mental images, drawings1, sounds (e.g., claps), acting out situations, verbal explanations, expressions, or equations.

CCSS.MATH.CONTENT.1.OA.C.6 — Add and subtract within 20, demonstrating fluency for addition and subtraction within 10. Use strategies such as counting on; making ten (e.g., 8 + 6 = 8 + 2 + 4 = 10 + 4 = 14); decomposing a number leading to a ten (e.g., 13 - 4 = 13 - 3 - 1 = 10 - 1 = 9); using the relationship between addition and subtraction (e.g., knowing that 8 + 4 = 12, one knows 12 - 8 = 4); and creating equivalent but easier or known sums (e.g., adding 6 + 7 by creating the known equivalent 6 + 6 + 1 = 12 + 1 = 13).

CCSS.MATH.CONTENT.2.OA.B.2 — Fluently add and subtract within 20 using mental strategies.2 By end of Grade 2, know from memory all sums of two one-digit numbers.

CCSS.MATH.CONTENT.3.OA.A.3 — Use multiplication and division within 100 to solve word problems in situations involving equal groups, arrays, and measurement quantities, e.g., by using drawings and equations with a symbol for the unknown number to represent the problem.1

CCSS.MATH.CONTENT.4.OA.B.4 — Find all factor pairs for a whole number in the range 1-100. Recognize that a whole number is a multiple of each of its factors. Determine whether a given whole number in the range 1-100 is a multiple of a given one-digit number. Determine whether a given whole number in the range 1-100 is prime or composite.

ELL Accommodations

Sentence stems
Peer turn and talk
Think, pair, share
Group work
Extra time for responses
Rephrase, repeat, or slow down
Drawing or model representation
Visuals and verbal cues to reinforce spoken and written language
Hands-on activities
Non-verbal responses
Manipulatives and counters

SPED Accommodations

Sentence stems
Practice making 10
Encouragement and assistance with selecting objects
Assistance with manipulating small objects
Additional time for completion
Breaks/PEAS area
Rephrase, repeat, or slow down
Drawing or model representation
Visuals and verbal cues
Visual schedule
Pre-teach vocabulary

Geometric Patterns in Our Natural World

For items in blue, scan the code or visit
tinyurl.com/EZPZ-Math-2

OBJECTIVES

- Students practice recognizing symmetry, angles, polygons, and other geometric forms as observable patterns in nature.

- Students classify different shapes and objects found in nature into mathematical and geometric concepts.

- Students visually represent mathematical and geometric patterns and objects found in nature.

- Students build upon a sense of camaraderie while cultivating classroom culture.

MATERIALS

- Clipboards
- Pencils
- Natural pattern pictures or other visuals
- Anchor Chart
- Geometry in Nature Exploration Guide

1 Set the Stage

- Begin with the **Big Question:** "Do you notice any patterns in nature?"

- Invite students to Turn and Talk, and think of some examples and share out. Spend 1 or 2 minutes on this.

- Present the **Big Idea:** "Math and geometry can help us understand the natural world."

- Introduce growth patterns to students and ask "What shapes are repeating in each pattern?" (Examples: spiral - curved line, branching - angles, tiling - intersecting lines, and explosion - one point and lines) Draw each growth pattern in real-time to illustrate the concept while also modeling what students will be doing today.

2 Breakout Procedure

- "Today we will have a scavenger hunt to search for these geometric patterns in nature. Complete your Exploration Guide by drawing or describing an example from nature for each geometric element you find while exploring outside." Have one example to show, such as a flower (radial symmetry), a snail shell (spiral), or a tree branch (branching).

- Review your outdoor learning expectations. Focus on safety when observing living organisms. Observe with eyes and do not handle organisms. Give clear spatial boundaries.

3 Explore

- Handout pencils and clipboards with the Geometry in Nature Exploration Guide.

- Invite students to search the outdoor area for these patterns. Students work independently but are invited to share their findings at the end of the activity.

- If students finish early, challenge them to work together to recreate these shapes and patterns with their bodies. (This serves as an extension of the lesson as well, either as preparation before the scavenger hunt or for deeper exploration after).

4 Reflect & Wrap-Up

- Call students back together and invite them to share if there was a pattern they were unable to find. Then ask other students to share if they were able to find that pattern.

- "Are there some geometric shapes you don't see very often in nature?" (Straight lines, right angles, squares, cubes, etc. Nature prefers round organic shapes.)

- "Are there some geometric shapes you see a lot?" (Radial symmetry, branching)

Math TEKS

K.6C — identify two-dimensional components of three-dimensional objects;

K.6D — identify attributes of two-dimensional shapes using informal and formal geometric language interchangeably;

K.6E — classify and sort a variety of regular and irregular two- and three-dimensional figures regardless of orientation or size; and

K.6F — create two-dimensional shapes using a variety of materials and drawings.

1.6A — classify and sort regular and irregular two-dimensional shapes based on attributes using informal geometric language;

1.6B — distinguish between attributes that define a two-dimensional or three-dimensional figure and attributes that do not define the shape;

1.6C — create two-dimensional figures, including circles, triangles, rectangles, and squares, as special rectangles, rhombuses, and hexagons;

1.6D — identify two-dimensional shapes, including circles, triangles, rectangles, and squares, as special rectangles, rhombuses, and hexagons and describe their attributes using formal geometric language;

1.6E — identify three-dimensional solids, including spheres, cones, cylinders, rectangular prisms (including cubes), and triangular prisms, and describe their attributes using formal geometric language;

2.8A — create two-dimensional shapes based on given attributes, including number of sides and vertices;

2.8B — classify and sort three-dimensional solids, including spheres, cones, cylinders, rectangular prisms (including cubes as special rectangular prisms), and triangular prisms, based on attributes using formal geometric language;

2.8C — classify and sort polygons with 12 or fewer sides according to attributes, including identifying the number of sides and number of vertices;

3.6A — classify and sort two- and three-dimensional figures, including cones, cylinders, spheres, triangular and rectangular prisms, and cubes, based on attributes using formal geometric language;

3.6B — use attributes to recognize rhombuses, parallelograms, trapezoids, rectangles, and squares as examples of quadrilaterals and draw examples of quadrilaterals that do not belong to any of these subcategories;

4.6B — identify and draw one or more lines of symmetry, if they exist, for a two-dimensional figure;

5.5 — Geometry and measurement. The student applies mathematical process standards to classify two dimensional figures by attributes and properties. The student is expected to classify two dimensional figures in a hierarchy of sets and subsets using graphic organizers based on their attributes and properties.

Common Core Standards

CCSS.MATH.KG.1 — Describe objects in the environment using names of shapes, and describe the relative positions of these objects using terms such as above, below, beside, in front of, behind, and next to.

CCSS.MATH.1.2 — Compose two-dimensional shapes (rectangles, squares, trapezoids, triangles, half-circles, and quarter-circles) or three-dimensional shapes (cubes, right rectangular prisms, right circular cones, and right circular cylinders) to create a composite shape, and compose new shapes from the composite shape.

CCSS.MATH.2.2 — Recognize and draw shapes having specialized attributes, such as a given number of angles or a given number of equal faces. Identify triangles, quadrilaterals, pentagons, hexagons, and cubes.

CCSS.MATH.3.1 — Understand that shapes in different categories (e.g., rhombuses, rectangles, and others) may share attributes (e.g., having four sides), and that the shared attributes can de ne a larger category (e.g., quadrilaterals). Recognize rhombuses, rectangles, and squares as examples of quadrilaterals, and draw examples of quadrilaterals that do not belong to any of these subcategories.

CCSS.MATH.4.2 — Classify two-dimensional figures based on the presence or absence of parallel or perpendicular lines, or the presence or absence of angles of a specialized size. Recognize right triangles as a category, and identify right triangles. (Two-dimensional shapes should include special triangles, e.g., equilateral, isosceles, scalene, and special quadrilaterals, e.g., rhombus, square, rectangle, parallelogram, trapezoid.)

CCSS.MATH.5.3 — Understand that attributes belonging to a category of two-dimensional figures also belong to all subcategories of that category. For example, all rectangles have four right angles and squares are rectangles, so all squares have four right angles.

CCSS.MATH.5.4 — Classify two-dimensional figures in a hierarchy based on properties.

ELL Accommodations

Sentence stems
Peer turn and talk (Think, pair, share)
Extra time for responses
Gestures for new vocabulary
Rephrase, repeat, or slow down
Drawing or model representation
Pre-teach vocabulary
Visuals and verbal cues to reinforce spoken and written language
Graphic organizers
Hands-on activities
Non-verbal responses
Group work

SPED Accommodations

Sentence stems
Assistance with scavenger hunt
Encouragement and assistance with selecting objects
Assistance with drawing objects
Scribing
Additional time for completion
Breaks/PEAS area
Rephrase, repeat, or slow down
Drawing or model representation
Visuals and verbal cues
Visual schedule
Pre-teach vocabulary

© 2023 Partners for Education, Agriculture, and Sustainability

Insect Census

For items in blue, scan the code or visit
tinyurl.com/EZPZ-Science-1

OBJECTIVES

- Students understand the basic parts and life stages of insects.
- Students understand that insects make up a large portion of living organisms on Earth.
- Students understand the diversity of insect species in their local habitat.

MATERIALS

— Hand lenses
— Clipboards
— Pencils
— Whiteboard or chart tablet
— Insect Parts and Stages Poster
— Insect Census Exploration Guide
— Optional: Insect Field Guides or other means of identification

1 Set the Stage

- Display Insect Parts and Stages Poster.
- Begin with the **Big Idea:** "There are more than one million known species of insects!"
- Present the **Big Question:** "What are examples of insects?"
- Discuss organisms commonly misidentified as insects: snails, worms, roly-polies, and spiders. You may choose to allow these other organisms in your census, but make the distinction between insects (3 body parts, 6 legs, and 2 antennae) and these other organisms. If you don't know what the other organisms are, this is a great opportunity for student research and leadership.
- Introduce the concept of a census. Give examples of what information a census can capture. Discuss what are the benefits of taking this data. Prompt students to predict where there may be inaccuracies or shortcomings in this form of data collection.

2 Breakout Procedure

- Introduce the Insect Census Exploration Guide. Read through the prompts on the sheet and check for understanding.
- Explain: "Your illustration should be as accurate as possible. What do you really see? Add as many details as you can."

3 Explore

- Students will wander through the outdoor learning area in search of insects.
- Once they have found an insect, they will draw it and label its parts on the Exploration Guide.
- Following the prompts on the Exploration Guide, students will describe their insect with words, identify its stage of life, use tally marks to count how many were observed, and consult with three peers to confirm identification.

4 Reflect & Wrap-Up

- Call students back together.
- Regroup. Have students put away tools and materials.
- Invite students to turn and talk, sharing something they learned about their insect.
- Teacher will add census data to a whiteboard or chart tablet.
- Closing questions: "Do you think we found all the insects in our outdoor area? Are there any insects that were not found that may visit our outdoor area during a different season or time of day? How might an insect census be useful to a farmer or gardener?"

Science TEKS

K.10B — identify basic parts of plants and animals

1.10D — observe and record life cycles of animals such as a chicken, frog, or fish.

2.10C — investigate and record some of the unique stages that insects such as grasshoppers and butterflies undergo during their life cycle.

3.9A — observe and describe the physical characteristics of environments and how they support populations and communities of plants and animals within an ecosystem

4.10C — explore, illustrate, and compare life cycles in living organisms such as beetles, crickets, radishes, or lima beans.

5.9A — observe the way organisms live and survive in their ecosystem by interacting with the living and nonliving components.

NGSS

2-LS4-1 — Make observations of plants and animals to compare the diversity of life in different habitats.

3-LS4-3 — Construct an argument with evidence that in a particular habitat some organisms can survive well, some survive less well, and some cannot survive at all.

ELL Accommodations

Sentence stems
Peer turn and talk
Think, pair, share
Extra time for responses
Rephrase, repeat, or slow down
Drawing or model representation
Visuals and verbal cues to reinforce spoken and written language
Hands-on activities
Group work

SPED Accommodations

Sentence stems
Scribing
Additional time for assignments/responses
Encouragement and assistance with insect Interactions
Breaks/PEAS area
Rephrase, repeat, or slow down
Drawing or model representation

© 2023 Partners for Education, Agriculture, and Sustainability

Solar Shadows

OBJECTIVES

- Students explore light energy in the garden.
- Students understand that solar energy travels in packets of energy called photons.
- Students explore how matter interacts with light from the sun.

MATERIALS

— Beach ball and marble; or other objects to represent the Sun and Earth.

— Clipboards, paper, pencils

1 Set the Stage

- **Big Idea:** "The Earth and the Sun are 94 million miles apart!" Use two round objects to represent the Sun (beach ball or balloon) and Earth (marble or pebble).

- Explain that the Earth is so far from the Sun that it actually takes light 8 minutes and 20 seconds to reach Earth from the Sun.

- Describe how light energy travels in small packets of electromagnetic radiation called photons.

- **Big Question:** "What happens when the Sun's light interacts with solid matter?"

2 Breakout Procedure

- Lead the students one step away from the "Sun" for each 1 million miles. Walk students 94 steps and then show them a marble or pebble representing Earth to give an idea of the distance and scale.

- Return to the gathering area.

- Explain that today they will try to capture what it looks like when a plant blocks a photon's path. Each student will trace the shadow made by a plant (or other object if necessary) from the garden. Model how to do this accurately and how not to let your own shadow get in the way.

3 Explore

- Students bring clipboards, paper, and pencils into the garden to try to trace a plant or other object's shadow.

4 Reflect & Wrap-Up

- Call students back together.
- Regroup. Ask: "What happened to the light energy before it reached their paper? What would happen if the moon was blocking the Sun?"
- Invite students to Turn and Talk, sharing something they learned about how photons interact with the object they drew.
- Closing questions: "How else does the energy from the Sun interact with life on Earth?"

5 Extension

- Allow students to brainstorm different systems that require energy from the Sun's photons. Examples may include water cycles, food chains, and ocean temperatures.
- Have students write an informational paragraph or essay describing how blocking sunlight could be used to mitigate climate change.

Science TEKS

K.6A — use the senses to explore different forms of energy such as light, thermal, and sound;

1.6A — identify and discuss how different forms of energy such as light, thermal, and sound are important to everyday life;

2.6A — investigate the effects on objects by increasing or decreasing amounts of light, heat, and sound energy such as how the color of an object appears different in dimmer light or how heat melts butter;

3.6A — explore different forms of energy, including mechanical, light, sound, and thermal in everyday life;

4.6A — differentiate among forms of energy, including mechanical, sound, electrical, light, and thermal;

5.6A — explore the uses of energy, including mechanical, light, thermal, electrical, and sound energy;

NGSS

K-PS3-1 — Make observations to determine the effect of sunlight on Earth's surface.

1-PS4-3 — Plan and conduct investigations to determine the effect of placing objects made with different materials in the path of a beam of light.

4-PS3-3 — Ask questions and predict outcomes about the changes in energy that occur when objects collide.

5-ESS1-1 — Support an argument that differences in the apparent brightness of the sun compared to other stars is due to their relative distances from the Earth.

ELL Accommodations

Sentence stems
Peer turn and talk
Think, pair, share
Extra time for responses
Gestures for new vocabulary
Rephrase, repeat, or slow down
Drawing or model representation
Pre-teach vocabulary
Graphic organizers
Non-verbal responses

SPED Accommodations

Sentence stems
Assistance with drawing
Additional time for assignments/responses
Breaks/PEAS area
Rephrase, repeat, or slow down
Drawing or model representation
Visuals and verbal cues
Pre-teach vocabulary

© 2023 Partners for Education, Agriculture, and Sustainability

Buzz, Buzz, Bees

OBJECTIVES

- Students understand that flowers are the seed-bearing part of a plant.
- Students understand that flower parts have specific names.
- Students understand why flowers are important to both plants and pollinators.
- Students understand the symbiotic relationship between some plants and pollinators.

1 Set the Stage

- Display parts of a flower poster and name key vocabulary: stem, sepals, petals, pistil, and stamen.
- Present the **Big Idea:** "Flowers are the seed-bearing part of a plant, consisting of reproductive parts that are often surrounded by brightly colored petals and green sepals."
- Ask the **Big Question:** "Why do plants have flowers?"
- Explain that pollination is how plants reproduce. It occurs when pollen from the male part of one flower travels to the female part of another flower where the seeds are made. New plants grow from the seeds that are created!
- Ask: "What do pollinators do?"
- Pollinators such as bees, insects, and birds do the important job of carrying pollen from one plant to another. Flowers attract pollinators using bright colors, smells, and a sugary liquid called nectar.

2 Breakout Procedure

- Explain that today we will be playing a game called Buzz, Buzz, Bees. We will be pretending that these cotton swabs are fuzzy bees. In this game, the students will be acting as bees and pretending to drink nectar by agitating as many flowers with their fuzzy bees (cotton swabs) as they can in 2 minutes.
- Model this action. Students must agitate each flower for 5 seconds (Counting aloud: one pollinator, two pollinator...) before moving on to the next flower.
- They will need to count in their head how many flowers they helped to pollinate.
- When completed they will find a friend and compare their numbers.
- You may want to do multiple rounds of this and challenge them to find different flowers this time. For example: "This round, only pollinate the blue and purple flowers. How many did you pollinate this time?" (These are the colors that bees can see and are attracted to the most!) "Next round, only pollinate the red flowers–these are the ones that hummingbirds prefer most."

MATERIALS

- Parts of a flower poster
- Clipboards, paper, and pencils
- Cotton swabs or felt bees glued to popsicle sticks
- Hand lenses
- Optional: Cut flowers my be used if there is not an abundance of flowers in the garden area.

Additional Resources:

See the Bee Cause information in Curriculum and Professional Development Resources section for more bee information and activities.

3 Explore

- Students play the game Buzz, Buzz, Bees.
- After they have compared numbers, they can move on to maintenance tasks: weeding, watering, mulching, and planting. Or, they may make a detailed drawing of their favorite flower.

4 Reflect & Wrap-Up

- Call students back together: "Little bees, little bees! Come back to your hive!". Challenge them to come back to the tarp or meeting area buzzing like a bee. Countdown from 5-4-3-2-1, all eyes and ears on you.
- Ask: "How can we help the bees and pollinators get more nectar?"
- Invite students to Turn and Talk, or share out to the group something they learned about parts of a flower or pollination.
- Ask the students what they learned about how we can help the pollinators and plants. What type of habitat is best for pollinators and plants?

Social Studies TEKS

K.10B — identify basic parts of plants and animals;

1.10B — identify and compare the parts of plants;

2.10B — observe, record, and compare how the physical characteristics of plants help them meet their basic needs such as stems carry water throughout the plant;

3.10A — explore how structures and functions of plants and animals allow them to survive in a particular environment;

4.10A — explore how structures and functions enable organisms to survive in their environment;

5.10A — compare the structures and functions of different species that help them live and survive in a specific environment such as hooves on prairie animals or webbed feet in aquatic animals;

NGSS

K-LS1-1 — Use observations to describe patterns of what plants and animals (including humans) need to survive.

1-LS1-1 — Use materials to design a solution to a human problem by mimicking how plants and/or animals use their external parts to help them survive, grow, and meet their needs.

2-LS2-2 — Develop a simple model that mimics the function of an animal in dispersing seeds or pollinating plants.

5-LS2-1 — Develop a model to describe the movement of matter among plants, animals, decomposers, and the environment.

ELL Accommodations

Sentence stems
Peer turn and talk
Think, pair, share
Extra time for responses
Gestures for new vocabulary
Rephrase, repeat, or slow down
Drawing or model representation
Pre-teach vocabulary
Visuals and verbal cues to reinforce spoken and written language
Hands-on activities

SPED Accommodations

Sentence stems
Assistance with drawing and navigating pollination game
Additional time for assignments/responses
Breaks/PEAS area
Rephrase, repeat, or slow down
Drawing or model representation
Visuals and verbal cues
Pre-teach vocabulary

Capture the Carbon

OBJECTIVES

- Students understand the role trees can play in mitigating climate change.
- Students understand the process by which trees remove atmospheric carbon from the air.
- Students understand the benefit of oxygen for many organisms.

MATERIALS

- Whiteboard or chart tablet
- Optional: Clay or playdough

Additional Resources:

Book: *Call Me Tree* by Maya Gonzales

Website: www.climate.mit.edu/ask-mit/how-do-greenhouse-gases-trap-heat-atmosphere

1 Set the Stage

- Begin with the **Big Idea:** "Trees help remove carbon from the air, which helps our planet stay healthy."
- **Big Question:** "How do trees remove carbon from the air?"
- Students can generate ideas while the teacher scribes them onto a whiteboard or chart tablet.
- Teacher describes the carbon cycle and explains that due to the burning of fossil fuels, there is an excess of carbon in our atmosphere. Carbon is called a greenhouse gas because it traps heat that would otherwise be released back into space like a greenhouse does for plants in the cool season.
- Students give responses and the teacher helps clarify the process by which trees remove and store carbon atoms from CO_2 and release the oxygen. Mention the benefits of oxygen for many organisms, including humans.
- "Today we will be playing a game to learn how trees can help remove atmospheric carbon and why that is good for the planet."

2 Breakout Procedure

Explain the rules of Capture the Carbon:

- One student starts as the tree, while the rest of the class forms groups of three representing CO_2.
- The game can be played as hide-and-seek or chase, where the tree finds the CO_2 groups and the first person touched is pulled off as the carbon atom and becomes part of the tree.
- The remaining two are now free oxygen atoms (Take a deep breath–Ahhh!) and can form another group of three if they can find a third person. The tree gets larger with each capture and must work to move together.
- The game continues until there are not enough children left to form a group of three.

3 Explore

- Explain any safety concerns and establish the boundaries before starting the game.
- Play Capture the Carbon for as long as desired. If students cannot find a third partner, it might be time for you to join the fun!
- When you are ready, call the students back together.

4 Reflect & Wrap-Up

- Challenge them to come back to the tarp or meeting area like softly drifting oxygen atoms. Countdown from 5-4-3-2-1, all eyes and ears on you.
- Optional: If materials are available and time allows, distribute two different colors of playdough to each student and have them form a CO2 molecule. One larger sphere (the carbon) with two smaller spheres (oxygen) stuck to its side. Once complete, the students will take turns pulling off the carbon and adding it together to form a tree sculpture. Once they are left with only oxygen you can have them take a big inhale of their leftover oxygen. It won't smell great but will probably get a big reaction!
- Invite students to Turn and Talk, or share out to the group something they learned about trees and their role in our environment.
- Ask the students what they learned about why trees are important.

Social Studies TEKS

K.8A — observe and describe weather changes from day to day and over seasons;

K.8B — identify events that have repeating patterns, including seasons of the year and day and night; and

K.8C — observe, describe, and illustrate objects in the sky such as the clouds, Moon, and Sun.

1.8A — record weather information, including relative temperature such as hot or cold, clear or cloudy, calm or windy, and rainy or icy;

1.8B — observe and record changes in the appearance of objects in the sky such as the Moon and stars, including the Sun;

1.8C — identify characteristics of the seasons of the year and day and night;

2.8A — measure, record, and graph weather information, including temperature, wind conditions, precipitation, and cloud coverage, in order to identify patterns in the data;

2.8B — identify the importance of weather and seasonal information to make choices in clothing, activities, and transportation;

3.8A — observe, measure, record, and compare day-to-day weather changes in different locations at the same time that include air temperature, wind direction, and precipitation;

4.8A — measure, record, and predict changes in weather;

4.8C — collect and analyze data to identify sequences and predict patterns of change in shadows, seasons, and the observable appearance of the Moon over time.

5.8A — differentiate between weather and climate;

NGSS

K-PS3-1 — Make observations to determine the effect of sunlight on Earth's surface.

1-PS4-3 — Plan and conduct investigations to determine the effect of placing objects made with different materials in the path of a beam of light.

4-PS3-2 — Make observations to provide evidence that energy can be transferred from place to place by sound, light, heat, and electric currents.

3-5-ETS1-1 — Define a simple design problem reflecting a need or a want that includes specified criteria for success and constraints on materials, time, or cost.

ELL Accommodations

Sentence stems	Rephrase, repeat, or slow down
Peer turn and talk	
Think, pair, share	Drawing or model representation
Extra time for responses	
Gestures for new vocabulary	Non-verbal responsesk

SPED Accommodations

Sentence stems	Breaks/PEAS area
Scribing	Rephrase, repeat, or slow down
Assistance with drawing	
Additional time for assignments/responses	Drawing or model representation
Encouragement and assistance with insect Interactions	Visuals and verbal cues
	Visual schedule
	Pre-teach vocabulary

© 2023 Partners for Education, Agriculture, and Sustainability

Advocacy in Action

For items in blue, scan the code or visit
tinyurl.com/EZPZ-RLA-1

OBJECTIVES

- Students understand the characteristics and purpose of argumentative text.
- Students understand that all living beings in a habitat are connected and subject to cause and effect.
- Students understand the human impact upon a habitat.

MATERIALS

- Clipboards
- Pencils
- Hand lenses
- Advocacy in Action Anchor Chart
- Argumentative Text Quick Write

1 Set the Stage

- Begin with the **Big Question:** "What is arguing? Can arguing be a good thing?"
- Invite students to Turn and Talk, and share about a time that they argued for something important. Remind them to give both partners a time to share and to use the sentence stem, "One time I argued because…"
- Bring the class back together to share out.
- Share the **Big Idea:** "When we make decisions for our community, people can disagree or debate. Leaders and decision makers in our community write argumentative texts to convince people of their ideas using claims, evidence, and explanations. Everyone here has experience arguing for something important, and you are all experts!"
- "Today we will write argumentative texts as nature advocates. Advocates are people who support or recommend decisions in our community by giving their opinions through argumentative texts. We will advocate for the living beings in this natural space."

2 Breakout Procedure

- Teacher says, "Imagine that this habitat which is home to many plants and animals is going to be destroyed and turned into a parking lot."
- Use empathy: "How would this feel if you were an ant or tree?"
- Explain to students they will create an argumentative text by listening and observing living beings in this space and use empathy to communicate the point of view of this living being in order to make a claim, provide evidence, and explain on their behalf.
- The teacher finds a living being and uses the Argumentative Text Quick Write to model listening, observing, and then using empathy to fill out the Quick Write from the living being's point of view. Remind students to use first person voice!
- Review your outdoor learning expectations. Focus on safety when observing organisms with hand lenses.
- Provide students the option to work in groups and give parameters for working collaboratively and sharing the work and ideas.

3 Explore

- Hand out pencils, hand lenses, and clipboards with Argumentative Text Quick Write.

- Invite students to explore their surroundings to choose an organism for whom they would like to advocate.

- After 15 minutes, if students have not started filing in their Argumentative Text Quick Write, invite them to begin so that they will have material to present to their community.

- Students work in groups or independently to complete the Quick Write. Students may have the option to fill out sentence stems on the handout or to freely compose their argument.

- Invite early finishers to draw or complete another Argumentative Text Quick Write with another living being.

4 Reflect & Wrap-Up

- Call students back together.

- Invite students to present their arguments for not destroying this habitat. Provide the option for students to read aloud in imagined voices of their living organisms.

- Closing question: "Why is nature advocacy important? How can we protect and advocate for living organisms in our own lives?"

Language Arts TEKS

K.7B — identify and describe the main character(s);

K.7D — describe the setting

K.11A — dictate or compose literary texts, including personal narratives; and

K.11B — dictate or compose informational texts

1.7A — describe personal connections to a variety of sources;

1.7B — write brief comments on literary or informational texts;

1.11A — plan a first draft by generating ideas for writing such as by drawing and brainstorming;

2.7A — describe personal connections to a variety of sources;

2.7E — interact with sources in meaningful ways such as illustrating or writing;

2.7F — respond using newly acquired vocabulary as appropriate.

2.11A — plan a first draft by generating ideas for writing such as drawing and brainstorming

2.12A — compose literary texts, including personal narratives and poetry;

3.7A — describe personal connections to a variety of sources, including self-selected texts;

3.7E — interact with sources in meaningful ways such as notetaking, annotating, freewriting, or illustrating;

3.7F — respond using newly acquired vocabulary as appropriate; and

3.11A — plan a first draft by selecting a genre for a particular topic, purpose, and audience using a range of strategies such as brainstorming, freewriting, and mapping;

3.12C — compose argumentative texts, including opinion essays, using genre characteristics and craft;

4.7A — describe personal connections to a variety of sources, including self-selected texts;

4.7E — interact with sources in meaningful ways such as notetaking, annotating, freewriting, or illustrating;

4.7F — respond using newly acquired vocabulary as appropriate;

4.11A — plan a first draft by selecting a genre for a particular topic, purpose, and audience using a range of strategies such as brainstorming, freewriting, and mapping;

4.12C — compose argumentative texts, including opinion essays, using genre characteristics and craft;

5.7A — describe personal connections to a variety of sources, including self-selected texts;

5.7E — interact with sources in meaningful ways such as notetaking, annotating, freewriting, or illustrating;

5.7F — respond using newly acquired vocabulary as appropriate;

5.11A — plan a first draft by selecting a genre for a particular topic, purpose, and audience using a range of strategies such as brainstorming, freewriting, and mapping;

5.12C — compose argumentative texts, including opinion essays, using genre characteristics and craft; and

Common Core Standards

CCSS.ELA-Literacy.W.3.1. — Write opinion pieces on topics or texts, supporting a point of view with reasons. a. Introduce the topic or text they are writing about, state an opinion, and create an organizational structure that lists reasons. b. Provide reasons that support the opinion. c. Use linking words and phrases (e.g., because, therefore, since, for example) to connect opinion and reasons. d. Provide a concluding statement or section.

CCSS.ELA-Literacy.W.4.1. — Write opinion pieces on topics or texts, supporting a point of view with reasons and information. a. Introduce a topic or text clearly, state an opinion, and create an organizational structure in which related ideas are grouped to support the writer's purpose. b. Provide reasons that are supported by facts and details. c. Link opinion and reasons using words and phrases (e.g., for instance, in order to, in addition). d. Provide a concluding statement or section related to the opinion presented.

CCSS.ELA-Literacy.W.4.1 — Write opinion pieces on topics or texts, supporting a point of view with reasons and information. a. Introduce a topic or text clearly, state an opinion, and create an organizational structure in which ideas are logically grouped to support the writer's purpose. b. Provide logically ordered reasons that are supported by facts and details. c. Link opinion and reasons using words, phrases, and clauses (e.g., consequently, specifically). d. Provide a concluding statement or section related to the opinion presented.

ELL Accommodations

Sentence stems
Peer turn and talk (think pair share)
Extra time for responses
Gestures for new vocabulary
Rephrase, repeat, or slow down
Pre-teach vocabulary
Visuals and verbal cues to reinforce spoken and written language
Graphic organizers
Hands-on activities
Group work

SPED Accommodations

Sentence stems
Graphic organizers
Use of computers or scribe
Shortened assignment
Additional time for completion
Breaks/PEAS area
Rephrase, repeat, or slow down
Drawing or model representation
Visuals and verbal cues
Visual schedule
Pre-teach vocabulary

Fibonacci Poetry

For items in blue, scan the code or visit
tinyurl.com/EZPZ-RLA-2

OBJECTIVES

- Students compose poetry texts, using genre characteristics and craft.
- Students notice patterns in nature.
- Students identify and apply rules of the Fibonacci series.

1 Set the Stage

- Teacher passes around objects such as small tree branches, pine cones, and shells. Teacher asks students the **Big Question:** "What patterns do you see in these objects? What patterns have you seen outdoors?"

- Teacher introduces the **Big Idea:** "The Fibonacci series or Golden Ratio is a pattern we see in nature. This pattern repeats forever and can be seen in many different places, such as shells, tree branches, flower petals, and even outer space! Let's make the Fibonacci series together!"

- As a class, students work in groups to create the first five numbers of the Fibonacci sequence. Teacher hands out sticks. Teacher guides students in the first six to seven numbers of the series and explains the pattern. "Each new number in the sequence is the combination of the two numbers before it. The first number is zero in the sequence, there is one zero and now we put one stick. One stick plus zero equals one, put another stick. Now the one stick and the one stick before it equal two. Two sticks and one stick equal three sticks. How many sticks are next if we combine the last two numbers of sticks? Two and three equal five sticks, so put five sticks down. With your partner, determine the next number of sticks. Eight sticks is correct because it is the sum of three and five sticks. This pattern repeats forever."

2 Breakout Procedure

- Teacher models writing a poem following the Fibonacci sequence.
- Teacher may use syllables or words that follow the pattern.
- Teacher models the incorporation of poetry characteristics such as rhythm, alliteration, and descriptive language as desired.
- Teacher invites students to visually construct a poem in a spiral, branch, or other representation of the Fibonacci sequence that they observed in nature.
- Model writing six or seven lines of poetry.
- Pass out various writing utensils and remind students to kindly share.
- Welcome collaboration and problem-solving among the students.

MATERIALS

- Artifacts containing Fibonacci series, such as small tree branches, snail shells, and pine cones.
- Small sticks or pebbles for students to use as manipulatives
- Chart paper
- Sharpie or marker
- Hand lenses
- Notebooks
- Pencils
- Anchor Chart

FIBONACCI POEM EXAMPLE

1,1	Seeds, seeds!
2,3,5	Spiral, secretly, mysteriously
8	Tied to the golden code of life
13	programmed from the cosmos unbreakable, infinite

© 2023 Partners for Education, Agriculture, and Sustainability

3 Explore

- Students explore space to find Fibonacci poetry in nature (minimum 15 minutes).
- Provide safety guidelines and physical boundaries of exploration.
- Students utilize hand lenses and make drawings to record observations of patterns in nature.
- After 15 minutes of exploration, invite students to construct their own Fibonacci pattern through poetry.
- Students write poems with Fibonacci patterns of syllables or words.
- If students finish early, students create their own Fibonacci art with found objects in nature. Remind students to not pick any leaves that are still alive.

4 Reflect & Wrap-Up

- Students return to the group.
- Invite students to share poems in the whole group, partners, or small groups.
- Teacher poses reflection questions at the end of the lesson:
  — "In your exploration, did you notice any representations of the Fibonacci sequence?"
  — "How did it feel to write in this pattern?"

Language Arts TEKS

K.11A — dictate or compose literary texts, including personal narratives;

1.12A — dictate or compose literary texts, including personal narratives and poetry;

2.12A — compose literary texts, including personal narratives and poetry;

3.12A — compose literary texts, including personal narratives and poetry, using genre characteristics and craft;

4.12A — compose literary texts such as personal narratives and poetry using genre characteristics and craft;

5.12A — compose literary texts such as personal narratives, fiction, and poetry using genre characteristics and craft;

Math TEKS

K.2A — count forward and backward to at least 20 with and without objects;

K.5E — create and use representations to organize, record, and communicate mathematical ideas;

K.5F — analyze mathematical relationships to connect and communicate mathematical ideas; and

K.5G — display, explain, and justify mathematical ideas and arguments using precise mathematical language in written or oral communication.

1.3D — apply basic fact strategies to add and subtract within 20, including making 10 and decomposing a number leading to a 10

2.4A — recall basic facts to add and subtract within 20 with automaticity;

3.5A — represent one- and two-step problems involving addition and subtraction of whole numbers to 1,000 using pictorial models, number lines, and equations

Common Core Reading Standards

CCSS.ELA-Literacy.RL.3.7. — Explain how specific aspects of a text's illustrations contribute to what is conveyed by the words in a story (e.g., create mood, emphasize aspects of a character or setting).

4TH GRADE

CCSS.ELA-Literacy.RL.4.7. — Make connections between the text of a story or drama and a visual or oral presentation of the text, identifying where each version reflects specific descriptions and directions in the text.

CCSS.ELA-Literacy.RL.5.7. — Analyze how visual and multimedia elements contribute to the meaning, tone, or beauty of a text (e.g., graphic novel, multimedia presentation of fiction, folktale, myth, poem).

Common Core Speaking and Listening Standards

CCSS.ELA-Literacy.SL.3.5. — Create engaging audio recordings of stories or poems that demonstrate fluid reading at an understandable pace; add visual displays when appropriate to emphasize or enhance certain facts or details.

CCSS.ELA-Literacy.SL.4.5. — Add audio recordings and visual displays to presentations when appropriate to enhance the development of main ideas or themes.

CCSS.ELA-Literacy.SL.5.5. — Include multimedia components (e.g., graphics, sound) and visual displays in presentations when appropriate to enhance the development of main ideas or themes.

Common Core Speaking and Listening Standards

CCSS.ELA-Literacy.W.3.4. — With guidance and support from adults, produce writing in which the development and organization are appropriate to task and purpose. (Grade-specific expectations for writing types are defined in standards 1–3 above.)

CCSS.ELA-Literacy.W.4.4 — Produce clear and coherent writing in which the development and organization are appropriate to task, purpose, and audience. (Grade-specific expectations for writing types are defined in standards 1–3 above.)

CCSS.ELA-Literacy.SL.5.4. — Produce clear and coherent writing in which the development and organization are appropriate to task, purpose, and audience. (Grade-specific expectations for writing types are defined in standards 1–3 above.)

ELL Accommodations

Sentence stems
Peer turn and talk (think pair share)
Extra time for responses
Gestures for new vocabulary
Rephrase, repeat, or slow down
Drawing or model representation
Pre-teach vocabulary
Visuals and verbal cues to reinforce spoken and written language
Hands-on activities
Non-verbal responses

SPED Accommodations

Sentence stems
Graphic organizers
Use of computers or scribe
Rhyming dictionary, thesaurus, or other resources
Shortened assignment
Additional time for completion
Breaks/PEAS area
Rephrase, repeat, or slow down
Drawing or model representation
Visuals and verbal cues
Visual schedule
Pre-teach vocabulary

© 2023 Partners for Education, Agriculture, and Sustainability

Sycamore Snake Mosaic

For items in blue, scan the code or visit
tinyurl.com/EZPZ-Art-1

OBJECTIVES

- Students explore differences and similarities within our Earth Family.

- Students understand that all living beings experience physical changes as we grow over time.

- Students understand that a mosaic is an arrangement of diverse elements forming a whole picture.

MATERIALS

- Side-by-side visual aid
- Cardstock paper
- Harvested sycamore tree bark
- Bins or trays for tree bark
- Clipboards (to secure cards outdoors)
- Pencils
- Crayons, colored pencils
- Liquid glue
- Model of completed Sycamore Snake Mosaic

1 Set the Stage

- Place hands together and say, "When I say, 'Hiss, Hiss,' you say 'I'm Ready for Thisssss!'" Slither arms like a snake.

- Display a poster with a side-by-side visual of a sycamore tree and a snake.

- Begin with the **Big Question:** "How are these two living beings different? How are they similar?"

- Present the **Big Idea:** "It is natural and perfectly normal for living beings of all kinds to shed layers." Whether those layers be skin, bark, leaves, fur or an exoskeleton. Many of us know that snakes shed their skin as they grow. Much like our baby clothes are too tight for us now, the snake outgrows its smaller layer of skin. Shedding this continuous layer of skin (ecdysis) helps snakes to remain happy and healthy, protecting them from harmful parasites and diseases as they grow bigger.

- Introduce the natural shedding of the sycamore trees by passing out the bins containing the outer bark. Allow a few minutes for the students to observe. Expect and celebrate any scales of bark becoming fragmented. If time allows, for personal connection, outdoor educators could ask students if they know of any other living things that shed their skin.

- "Hiss, hiss!"— "I'm Ready for Thisssss!" Invite students to bring their hands to their laps and refocus as they listen to some fun facts in preparation for the art craft.

- Discuss that as the sycamore tree grows, the inner cambium layer (the moist green layer responsible for trunk growth) expands, causing the old bark to drop off. This is similar to the snake outgrowing its smaller skin to stay healthy and strong. Behind these sheets of exfoliated bark, a new creamy white growth layer is exposed. Shedding is a sign of optimal health of the sycamore tree.

2 Breakout Procedure

- Introduce the model of a Sycamore Snake Mosaic. Teacher models: "First, I drew the snake. Then, I colored the bark. Last, I glued the bark on the cardstock snake design."

- Be open to the students finding their own way through the process

- Remind students that the bark breaks easily: "That's okay, Sycamore!"

- Help students connect how snakes have patterns or different colors on their scales that tell us about them (diamondbacks/ brightly colored coral snakes/garden snakes are green for camouflage). Invite students to consider these things as well to further push imagination.

- Gently split bark over the containers. If any breaks during coloring, assure them it will add more beauty to their mosaics.

- Remind students, "Dot, dot, not a lot" when using liquid glue.

- Explain that today we will become new animals living in an ecosystem community.

- Show students the "Wise Grand Owl" Nature Name Tag as a reference, "Notice how I wrote my nature name and I drew a picture."

- Invite students to imagine their own drawing and Nature Name: First, Middle, and Last (this ensures a variety of names even if there are several of the same favorite animal).

- Pass out clipboards with attached index cards.

- Pass out various writing utensils and remind students to kindly share.

- Welcome collaboration and problem-solving among the students.

3 Explore

- Pass out clipboards with cardstock. Set out glue with various pencils at their creation stations.

- Invite students to begin once they have their clipboard and pencils

- While they create, celebrate their unique styles with the following affirming prompts:
  - "I am here to help you if you feel frustrated about something."
  - "I love the idea that you came up with and how it is different from mine."
  - "I am excited for you to take your creation home with you."

- Students who finish early may set their craft to dry in a designated area and are invited to offer their friends help or sit together to share their completed mosaics with one another.

Art TEKS

K.2A — create artworks using a variety of lines, shapes, colors, textures, and forms;

K.2B — arrange components intuitively to create artworks; and

K.2C — use a variety of materials to develop manipulative skills while engaging in opportunities for exploration through drawing, painting

1.2A — invent images that combine a variety of lines, shapes, colors, textures, and forms;

1.2B — place components in orderly arrangements to create designs; and

1.2C — increase manipulative skills necessary for using a variety of materials to produce drawings, paintings, prints, constructions, and sculptures, including modeled forms.

2.2A — express ideas and feelings in personal artworks using a variety of lines, shapes, colors, textures, forms, and space;

2.2B — create compositions using the elements of art and principles of design; and

2.2C — identify and practice skills necessary for producing drawings, paintings, prints, constructions, and sculpture, including modeled forms, using a variety of materials.

3.2A — integrate ideas drawn from life experiences to create original works of art;

3.2B — create compositions using the elements of art and principles of design; and

3.2C — produce drawings; paintings; prints; sculpture, including modeled forms; and other art forms such as ceramics, fiber art, constructions, mixed media, installation art, digital art and media, and photographic imagery using a variety of materials.

4.2A — integrate ideas drawn from life experiences to create original works of art;

4.2B — create compositions using the elements of art and principles of design; and

4.2C — produce drawings; paintings; prints; sculpture, including modeled forms; and other art forms such as ceramics, fiber art, constructions, mixed media, installation art, digital art and media, and photographic imagery using a variety of art media and materials.

5.2A — integrate ideas drawn from life experiences to create original works of art;

5.2B — create compositions using the elements of art and principles of design; and

5.2C — produce drawings; paintings; prints; sculpture, including modeled forms; and other art forms such as ceramics, fiber art, constructions, digital art and media, and photographic imagery using a variety of materials.

© 2023 Partners for Education, Agriculture, and Sustainability

4 Reflect & Wrap-Up

- "Hiss, Hiss" call and response, then provide students with a 5-minute notice.

- Call students back together. "Let's give each other a round of applause!" Acknowledge how proud you are of their creations.

- Ask: "How did we show respect to the sycamore tree today?"

- If time allows, encourage students to browse around (like an art exhibit) and compliment each other's artwork.

5 Extension

- For deeper exploration, a tarp can be spread out for seating and this lesson can be introduced near a shedding sycamore tree. Bark can then be harvested by students.

- Mosaics can be created with fallen leaves, seed pod casings, or various bark types if sycamore trees or bark sheets are not accessible. The goal is to sustainably collect what has been naturally shed or dropped off from trees or plants.

- There is an opportunity to invite students to collaborate on a poster-sized mosaic as a rainy-day variation.

ELL Accommodations

Sentence stems
Graphic organizers
Peer turn and talk
Think, pair, share
Extra time for responses
Gestures for new vocabulary
Rephrase, repeat, or slow down
Drawing or model representation
Pre-teach vocabulary
Visuals and verbal cues to reinforce spoken and written language
Hands-on activities
Non-verbal responses

SPED Accommodations

Sentence stems
Graphic organizers
Assistance with handling sycamore bark
Multiple attempts if bark breaks
Markers instead of colored pencils if needed
Additional time for completion
Breaks/PEAS area
Rephrase, repeat, or slow down
Drawing or model representation
Visuals and verbal cues
Visual schedule
Pre-teach vocabulary

Pod PEAple

OBJECTIVES

- Students understand that the size of different objects is relative.
- Students understand that looking closely can reveal unknown or unexpected information.
- Students understand that real-life experience can inform your art.

1 Set the Stage

- Display a poster with a simple map of your outdoor learning space.
- Begin with the **Big Question:** "Does the world look different based on your relative size?"
- Present the **Big Idea:** "We can explore different perspectives through our art."
- Introduce the concept that size is relative. We may be very big compared to an ant, but we are quite little next to a humpback whale. Your size is different compared to different objects or organisms.
- Have the students describe some things they consider very big and some they think of as tiny. Write down on chart paper or whiteboard the items that the students share under the titles: **Big** and **Small.**
- Optional: Read a text about paying close attention or the size of objects, such as *Look Closer* by Rebecca Wildsmith or *Actual Size* by Steve Jenkins

2 Breakout Procedure

- Explain that today we are going to shrink down to a very small size. Students will be given a small ball of clay or playdough. They will use this to sculpt a tiny version of themselves.
- If it is helpful, provide rulers or nonstandard forms of measurement (a length of yarn or a stick) and instruct that the little self they create cannot be taller than a certain length.
- Once the little selves are complete, the Outdoor Education Specialist can say the magic words: "Bippity-boppity, *alakazeeple...* Turn these students into *Pod PEAple!*"

MATERIALS

- Clay or Play-Doh
- Plastic trays or paper plates
- Hand lenses
- Paper, pencils, and clipboards
- Optional: Rulers
- Optional: Art supplies (watercolors, paints, brushes)

© 2023 Partners for Education, Agriculture, and Sustainability

3 Explore

- Once they have transformed into their little selves, students will be allowed to explore the garden as tiny people.
- Encourage them to use their little clay selves to explore and use hand lenses to see things in greater detail.
- "Does it take longer to get somewhere when you are little? What things might be hazardous when you are little? Would garden vegetables provide more food for our little selves?"
- Remind students to use caution when exploring and follow all garden expectations.

4 Reflect & Wrap-Up

- Call students back together. Challenge them to fly their PEAple through the air! Countdown from 5-4-3-2-1, all eyes and ears on you.
- Have students share (if they feel comfortable) their stories with the group or with a friend.
- Remind students: "The world would look very different if you were that little. Thank goodness you are so big! I wonder what the world would look like if we were much, much bigger?"

5 Extension

- Complete a storytelling activity. Explain that you would like them to illustrate a comic book about their adventure in the garden.
- Remind them to try to draw and explain accurately the things they saw and experienced. The comic can be whatever they wish. Encourage them to use their imaginations.

Art TEKS

K.1A — gather information from subjects in the environment using the senses;

K.2C — use a variety of materials to develop manipulative skills while engaging in opportunities for exploration through drawing, painting, printmaking, constructing artworks, and sculpting, including modeled forms

1.1A — identify similarities, differences, and variations among subjects in the environment using the senses;

1.2C — increase manipulative skills necessary for using a variety of materials to produce drawings, paintings, prints, constructions, and sculptures, including modeled forms.

2.1A — compare and contrast variations in objects and subjects from the environment using the senses;

2.2C — identify and practice skills necessary for producing drawings, paintings, prints, constructions, and sculpture, including modeled forms, using a variety of materials

3.1A — explore ideas from life experiences about self, peers, family, school, or community and from the imagination as sources for original works of art;

3.2C — produce drawings; paintings; prints; sculpture, including modeled forms; and other art forms such as ceramics, fiber art, constructions, mixed media, installation art, digital art and media, and photographic imagery using a variety of materials

4.1A — explore and communicate ideas drawn from life experiences about self, peers, family, school, or community and from the imagination as sources for original works of art;

4.2C — produce drawings; paintings; prints; sculpture, including modeled forms; and other art forms such as ceramics, fiber art, constructions, mixed media, installation art, digital art and media, and photographic imagery using a variety of art media and materials.

5.1A — develop and communicate ideas drawn from life experiences about self, peers, family, school, or community and from the imagination as sources for original works of art;

5.2C — produce drawings; paintings; prints; sculpture, including modeled forms; and other art forms such as ceramics, fiber art, constructions, digital art and media, and photographic imagery using a variety of materials.

Common Core: (Extension Activity)

CCSS.ELA-Literacy.W.K.3 — Use a combination of drawing, dictating, and writing to narrate a single event or several loosely linked events, tell about the events in the order in which they occurred, and provide a reaction to what happened.

CCSS.ELA-Literacy.W.1.3 — Write narratives in which they recount two or more appropriately sequenced events, include some details regarding what happened, use temporal words to signal event order, and provide some sense of closure.

CCSS.ELA-Literacy.W.2.3 — Write narratives in which they recount a well-elaborated event or short sequence of events, include details to describe actions, thoughts, and feelings, use temporal words to signal event order, and provide a sense of closure.

CCSS.ELA-Literacy.W.3.3 — Write narratives to develop real or imagined experiences or events using effective technique, descriptive details, and clear event sequences.

   a. Establish a situation and introduce a narrator and/or characters; organize an event sequence that unfolds naturally.

CCSS.ELA-Literacy.W.4.3 — Write narratives to develop real or imagined experiences or events using effective technique, descriptive details, and clear event sequences.

   a. Orient the reader by establishing a situation and introducing a narrator and/or characters; organize an event sequence that unfolds naturally.

CCSS.ELA-Literacy.W.5.3. — Write narratives to develop real or imagined experiences or events using effective technique, descriptive details, and clear event sequences.

   a. Orient the reader by establishing a situation and introducing a narrator and/or characters; organize an event sequence that unfolds naturally.

ELL Accommodations

Sentence stems
Peer turn and talk
Think, pair, share
Extra time for responses
Gestures for new vocabulary
Rephrase, repeat, or slow down
Drawing or model representation
Pre-teach vocabulary
Visuals and verbal cues to reinforce spoken and written language
Hands-on activities
Non-verbal responses

SPED Accommodations

Assistance with creating clay people
Assistance with extension activity (can provide paper with pre-drawn comic book frame)
Additional time for assignments/responses
Breaks/PEAS area
Rephrase, repeat, or slow down
Drawing or model representation
Visuals and verbal cues
Sentence stems
Pre-teach vocabulary

Drawing or model representation
Visuals and verbal cues
Visual schedule
Pre-teach vocabulary

© 2023 Partners for Education, Agriculture, and Sustainability

Music in the Wild

OBJECTIVES

- Students understand that cultures use natural resources to fashion instruments.

- Students understand that music is used to share history, wisdom, and build community.

- Students understand the diversity of natural materials used for potential instruments.

1 Set the Stage

- Demonstrate various instruments being played to gather your students' attention. If you are showing pictures, consider drumming with sticks, shaking seed pods, or using something from outdoors in your vicinity.

- Begin with the **Big Question:** "How is music made in nature?"

- Present the **Big Idea:** "Melodies and rhythms can be found in nature with birds, bees, whales, rain, wind, and through human-crafted instruments."

- Discuss how many instruments were created from found materials in nature. Many were designed to mimic the sounds of the natural world, such as rainsticks, or various hand-crafted rattles to represent the rain, or drums representing the heartbeat of life. Other instruments have even been designed to mimic sounds of animals in the wild. For example, Incan whistling pots, filled with water and shaped precisely, generate animal sounds when tilted or blown into.

- Discuss how group sound experiences continue to be used to give respect to the earth and build communities close to nature and one another. Whether that be through drumming while seed planting, playing nature-made rattles to call for rain, sounding a conch shell to the seven directions, or sharing in music to celebrate stories told through the generations.

2 Breakout Procedure

- "Demonstrate for students that they will be crafting their own musical instruments.

- Introduce the provided assortment of clay and other natural materials students may use to craft their own instruments.

- Explain to students that you have also provided materials for decoration, such as craft tape and paint markers.

- Review your outdoor boundaries.

- Invite students to explore the outdoor area to find any additional natural materials.

- Pass out various writing utensils and remind students to kindly share.

- Welcome collaboration and problem-solving among the students.

MATERIALS

- Examples or visual aids of natural instruments such as conch shells, gourds, rattles, stones of various textures, rainsticks, bamboo chimes, etc.

- Various shells and rattling seed pods

- Visual aid of ancient musical instruments if available

- Sticks and pebbles

- Paint markers

- Clay and craft tape

- Trash receptacle

3 Explore

- Invite students to begin exploring and selecting from the provided materials or those collected outdoors.
- Remind students: "This is not about perfection. Let's get creative!"
- While exploring, prompt with the following questions:
  - "Is your instrument inspired by an animal?"
  - "How do you predict your instrument will sound?"
  - "What materials did you choose for your instrument?"

4 Reflect & Wrap-Up

- Call students back together. Challenge them to keep rhythm with you as you all play your instruments.
- Use this opportunity to create a group rhythm or song.
- Ask: "What was it like to create your own instrument?"
- "Did it create a sound like the one you predicted?"
- "Will you continue to play this instrument?"
- "What changes would you make to your design?"

5 Extension

- Create future songs together to solidify information regarding other subject material.
- Host a performance for students' families.

Art TEKS

K.6C — distinguish between rhythms, higher/lower pitches, louder/softer dynamics, faster/slower tempos, and simple patterns in musical performances;

1.6C — distinguish same/different between beat/rhythm, higher/lower, louder/softer, faster/slower, and simple patterns in musical performances;

2.6C — distinguish between rhythms, higher/lower pitches, louder/softer dynamics, faster/slower tempos, and simple patterns in musical performances;

3.6C — identify specific musical events in aural examples such as changes in timbre, form, tempo, or dynamics using appropriate vocabulary;

4.6C — describe specific musical events in aural examples such as changes in timbre, form, tempo, dynamics, or articulation using appropriate vocabulary;

5.6C — describe specific musical events such as changes in timbre, form, tempo, dynamics, or articulation in aural examples using appropriate vocabulary;

ELL Accommodations

Sentence stems
Peer turn and talk
Think, pair, share
Extra time for responses
Gestures for new vocabulary
Rephrase, repeat, or slow down
Drawing or model representation
Pre-teach vocabulary
Visuals and verbal cues to reinforce spoken and written language
Hands-on activities
Non-verbal responses

SPED Accommodations

Assistance with creating musical instruments
Allow for breaks from loud music
Allow noise-canceling headphones or distance from loud noises
Additional time for assignments/responses
Breaks/PEAS area
Rephrase, repeat, or slow down
Drawing or model representation
Sentence stems
Visuals and verbal cues
Pre-teach vocabulary

Nature's Palette

For items in blue, scan the code or visit
tinyurl.com/EZPZ-Art-4

OBJECTIVES

- Students gather information from or in the environment using their senses.
- Students understand that organisms have complex and subtle color palettes.
- Students understand that knowledge of an organism's color palette can be used to make accurate scientific drawings.
- Students examine contemporary artworks.

MATERIALS

— Clipboards

— Paper

— Coloring tools such as colored pencils, crayons, and markers

— Nature's Palette Exploration Guide

— Optional: Hand lenses

1 Set the Stage

- Display an image of artwork by Juliet Whitsett.
- Describe the process of selecting the most prominent colors of a living organism and creating a color palette.
- Begin with the **Big Question:** "What colors can we observe in our outdoor environment?"
- **Big Idea:** "Living organisms exhibit a range of colors that we can use when making scientific drawings."

2 Breakout Procedure

- Introduce the Nature's Palette Exploration Guide.
- Explain that students will explore the garden, looking for a living thing.
- Once they have made their selection, they will complete the Exploration Guide by filling in the four most prominent colors and then use those colors to make a scientific drawing of their organism.

3 Explore

- Distribute clipboards and Nature's Palette Exploration Guide and allow the students to make their own choice of organism.
- Provide an assortment of coloring tools (colored pencils, crayons, markers) with which to create their palettes.

Art examples courtesy of Juliet Whitsett.

Juliet Whitsett (she/her) is an Austin, TX based Artist and Arts & Environmental Educator. Her interactive work and art series, Biodiversity of Texas, uses story-telling, engages empathy, and celebrates the incredible diversity and importance of species in her home state. With roughly ~150 threatened and ~75 endangered species in Texas alone, Juliet has been learning, creating art about and partnering with leading experts in order to share the importance of our world's biodiversity. Her digital, acrylic, and experiential audio art pieces aim to bring awareness to our rarest + most at risk species — those who obviously have no means of advocating for themselves. See more of her art series at
www.julietwhitsett.com

4 Reflect & Wrap-Up

- Call students back together. Challenge them to bend back to you like a rainbow! Countdown from 5-4-3-2-1, all eyes and ears on you.

- Invite students to share their color palette drawings in the whole group, partners, or small groups.

- Teacher poses reflection questions at the end of the lesson:
  - "How can we accurately draw organisms we encounter outdoors?"
  - "What are some patterns we noticed about colors in the garden?"

5 Extension

- Let the students brainstorm the different feelings and emotions associated with various colors: hot/cold, happy/sad, excited/calm, etc. Why is green so often found on plants? What emotions are associated with the color green and why?

- Write a personal narrative exploring a memory you have associated with one or more of the colors from your palette.

Art TEKS

K.1A — gather information from subjects in the environment using the senses; and

K.1B — identify the elements of art, including line, shape, color, texture, and form, and the principles of design, including repetition/pattern and balance, in the environment.

1.1A — identify similarities, differences, and variations among subjects in the environment using the senses; and

1.1B — identify the elements of art, including line, shape, color, texture, and form, and the principles of design, including emphasis, repetition/pattern, and balance, in nature and human-made environments.

2.3B — examine historical and contemporary artworks created by men and women, making connections to various cultures;

3.3B — compare and contrast artworks created by historical and contemporary men and women, making connections to various cultures;

4.3B — compare purpose and content in artworks created by historical and contemporary men and women, making connections to various cultures;

5.3B — compare the purpose and effectiveness of artworks created by historic and contemporary men and women, making connections to various cultures;

Common Core (Extension Activity)

CCSS.ELA-Literacy.W.K.1 — Use a combination of drawing, dictating, and writing to compose opinion pieces in which they tell a reader the topic or the name of the book they are writing about and state an opinion or preference about the topic or book

CCSS.ELA-Literacy.W.1.1 — Write opinion pieces in which they introduce the topic or name the book they are writing about, state an opinion, supply a reason for the opinion, and provide some sense of closure.

CCSS.ELA-Literacy.W.2.1 — Write opinion pieces in which they introduce the topic or book they are writing about, state an opinion, supply reasons that support the opinion, use linking words (e.g., because, and, also) to connect opinion and reasons, and provide a concluding statement or section.

CCSS.ELA-Literacy.W.3.1 — Write opinion pieces on topics or texts, supporting a point of view with reasons.

   a. Introduce the topic or text they are writing about, state an opinion, and create an organizational structure that lists reasons.

   b. Provide reasons that support the opinion.

CCSS.ELA-Literacy.W.4.1 — Write opinion pieces on topics or texts, supporting a point of view with reasons and information.

   a. Introduce a topic or text clearly, state an opinion, and create an organizational structure in which related ideas are grouped to support the writer's purpose.

   b. Provide reasons that are supported by facts and details.

© 2023 Partners for Education, Agriculture, and Sustainability

CCSS.ELA-Literacy.W.5.1 — Write opinion pieces on topics or texts, supporting a point of view with reasons and information.

a. Introduce a topic or text clearly, state an opinion, and create an organizational structure in which ideas are logically grouped to support the writer's purpose.

b. Provide logically ordered reasons that are supported by facts and details.

ELL Accommodations

Sentence stems
Graphic organizers
Peer turn and talk
Think, pair, share
Extra time for responses
Gestures for new vocabulary
Rephrase, repeat, or slow down
Drawing or model representation
Pre-teach vocabulary
Visuals and verbal cues to reinforce spoken and written language
Hands-on activities
Non-verbal responses

SPED Accommodations

Sentence stems
Graphic organizers
Assistance with art materials
Multiple attempts at color painting
Guidance exploring the garden
Additional time for completion
Breaks/PEAS area
Rephrase, repeat, or slow down
Drawing or model representation
Visuals and verbal cues
Visual schedule
Pre-teach vocabulary

Tasting Tour

For items in blue, scan the code or visit
tinyurl.com/EZPZ-Health-1

OBJECTIVES

- Students identify characteristics of edible plants through their senses.

- Students develop plant identification skills through smell, sight, texture, and taste.

- Students understand that plants can be grown as a source of food and nutrition.

1 Set the Stage

- Teacher displays the Sensory Anchor Chart. Materials for food serving are prepped and ready for students. Clipboards with sufficient copies of the Tasting Response Sheet are available for students.

- **Big Idea:** "Plants contain nutrients and minerals that are essential for human growth. Plants have distinct attributes that may influence which foods we prefer to eat."

- **Big Question:** "What are our five senses? How can they help us enjoy our foods? What about plants attracts us (for example: bees are attracted to different flowers)? What is nutrition? Why are nutrients important? Where do nutrients in our food come from? (Nutrients come from the soil and enter the plant with the help of water!)"

- Discuss: "Think about some different plants we have eaten before. Let's create a dance with our bodies of how some of these plants taste, smell or feel (its texture) in our mouth. For example, a lemon tastes sour in my mouth. For me, it's like being squeezed! What are some other foods that we can represent with dance?"

2 Breakout Procedure

- Teacher says: "Today you will be sampling some vegetables/herbs from our garden. We will pay close attention to the smell, sight, texture, and taste of each plant as we taste them."

- Respect our Flavor Identities (a.k.a. Don't yuck someone's yum). "Just like the games or toys that we enjoy, our favorite flavors are our own, and come from our experiences and memories. We will respect the likes and dislikes of everyone in our community."

MATERIALS

- Sampling of edible plants: mint, rosemary, basil, lemons, limes, kale, radishes, carrots, apples and/or any currently edible plants available from your outdoor area

- Clipboards

- Pencils

- Coloring materials

- Options for serving: sample cups, small plates, or napkins

- Hand sanitizer

- Bowl for washing produce

- Water for washing produce

- Knife or scissors

- Cutting board

- Tasting Response Sheet

- Sensory Anchor Chart

FOOD SAFETY

Ensure you are certified to serve and handle food products. This certification can be earned online and usually costs around $10.

© 2023 Partners for Education, Agriculture, and Sustainability

3 Explore

- Tasting Texture station: Students taste different produce and herbs and teacher informs students of their nutrients. While tasting plants, students will represent flavor and texture with their own dance for each plant. On their Tasting Response Sheets, students create an image that represents how the plant tasted and felt (texture) in their mouth. Invite students to use shapes, lines, and colors to describe plant taste and texture, along with descriptive words.

- Smell and Sight Station: Plant identification and plant rubbings: Students use pencils or other drawing materials to create rubbings of plants on paper. In groups, students discuss how plants look and smell from plant rubbings.

4 Reflect & Wrap-Up

- Students and teachers clean up and return to the whole group area.

- Teacher challenges students to do the dance of their favorite flavor back to the whole group area.

- Reflection questions:
  - "What senses did you use the most in our exploration time?"
  - "How did your senses help you enjoy the plants you tasted today?"

- Invite students to share the dance of the favorite plant they tasted.

Physical Education TEKS

K.10A — recognize that eating a variety of foods produces energy for physical activity;

1.10A — identify healthy foods that produce energy for physical activity;

2.10A — identify the types of food that produce energy to enhance physical activity;

3.10A — differentiate between healthy and unhealthy foods and their impact on sustainable energy for physical activity;

4.10A — examine the relationship between nutrition and optimal physical performance;

5.10A — identify healthy foods that enhance physical activity.

Common Core

CCSS.ELA-Literacy.W.K.2 — Use a combination of drawing, dictating, and writing to compose informative/explanatory texts in which they name what they are writing about and supply some information about the topic.

CCSS.ELA-Literacy.W.1.2 — Write informative/explanatory texts in which they name a topic, supply some facts about the topic, and provide some sense of closure.

CCSS.ELA-Literacy.W.2.2 — Write informative/explanatory texts in which they introduce a topic, use facts and definitions to develop points, and provide a concluding statement or section.

CCSS.ELA-Literacy.W.3.2 — Write informative/explanatory texts to examine a topic and convey ideas and information clearly.

> b. Develop the topic with facts, definitions, and details.

CCSS.ELA-Literacy.W.4.2 — Write informative/explanatory texts to examine a topic and convey ideas and information clearly

> b. Develop the topic with facts, definitions, concrete details, quotations, or other information and examples related to the topic.

CCSS.ELA-Literacy.W.5.2. — Write informative/explanatory texts to examine a topic and convey ideas and information clearly.

> b. Develop the topic with facts, definitions, concrete details, quotations, or other information and examples related to the topic.

ELL Accommodations

Sentence stems	representation
Peer turn and talk (think pair share)	Pre-teach vocabulary
Extra time for responses	Visuals and verbal cues to reinforce spoken and written language
Gestures for new vocabulary	
Rephrase, repeat, or slow down	Graphic organizer
	Hands-on activities
Drawing or model	Non-verbal responses

SPED Accommodations

Sentence stems	Breaks/PEAS area
Choice regarding which plants to smell, touch, and taste	Rephrase, repeat, or slow down
	Drawing or model representation
Hand or facial movements can substitute for dance if child has mobility issues	Visuals and verbal cues
	Visual schedule
Shortened assignment	Pre-teach vocabulary
Additional time for completion	Pre-teach vocabulary

Changes in Plants: Herbal Tea

For items in blue, scan the code or visit
tinyurl.com/EZPZ-Health-2

OBJECTIVES

- Students observe and record changes in water and plants when heated and cooled.
- Students explore and compare tea mixtures and solutions.
- Students understand the nutritional properties of different herbal teas, like hydration.

MATERIALS

- Electric kettle
- Large heat-resistant pitcher
- Thermometers for group work (5-10)
- Oven mitts
- Heat-resistant disposable cups
- Spoons (compostable or reusable)
- Trays
- Dried hibiscus flowers for tea
- Locally sourced herbs, such as mint and lemon balm
- Clipboards
- Pencils
- Strainer or empty tea filter bags
- Hand sanitizer
- Timer
- Optional: Tongs for group work (5-10)
- Optional: Honey or sugar
- Changes in Plants Anchor Chart
- Changes in Plants Exploration Guide

1 Set the Stage

- Teacher displays the Anchor Chart and has prepared and organized plant materials on trays. Tea kettle, pitcher of room temperature water, and tasting materials are ready and organized. Clipboards are ready with Exploration Guides.
- **Big Idea:** "When we heat a mixture of plants and water, we create a solution called tea. With heat, plants undergo a chemical change and release nutrients. These nutrients benefit our bodies in many different ways."
- **Big Question:** "How can heat change the physical properties of plants? Why do we use plants to make tea?"
- Teacher says: "For thousands of years in many parts of the world, people have used heat to unlock beneficial properties of plants. One way we do this is by making tea. We will explore how heat changes a mixture of water and plants into a solution also known as tea. Turn and talk with a partner. Share and/or listen to an experience with tea."
- Teacher introduces plants provided for tea and describes their taste and nutritional benefits. Teacher speaks to how tea is also a source of hydration because it is made of water.

2 Breakout Procedure

- Teacher says: "Today you will observe and compare the effects of heating matter by making tea. You will observe and explore with taste, touch, sight, and smell the properties of a plant and water mixture. This mixture, known as herbal tea, is a solution."
- Teacher breaks students into groups. Each group will get a tray with herb samplings, honey or sugar (optional), spoons, and two cups per student.

3 Explore

- Students explore and observe herbs on trays and record observations, sharing and writing in their Exploration Guides.

- Teacher sets a timer for 5 minutes.

- Students place their preferred herbs into their cups, with room temperature water and hot water in respective cups. Herbs may be placed in tea bags to make it easier for students to drink.

- Students observe and record temperature of water and changes in the physical properties of water and plants in the Exploration Guide.

- At the end of 5 minutes, students should remove their herbs by taking out the tea bag or straining their tea. Students are encouraged to taste cups with room temperature and hot water. Students will compare and record their observations of each liquid in their Exploration Guides.

4 Reflect & Wrap-Up

- Students clean up materials.

- Teacher calls students back to the whole group area.

- Reflection questions:
  - "How did heat change the plants and water in your cup?"
  - "Describe the tea you made with a partner. What would you add to your tea next time?"
  - "We drink tea to benefit our bodies and provide nutrients. Tea is also a source of hydration. What way would you like to use tea to help your body?"

Health TEKS

K.6C — identify types of foods that help the body grow, including fruits and vegetables, dairy, and protein;

1.6A — explain that fruits, proteins, vegetables, and dairy provide essential vitamins and minerals;

2.6A — identify types of nutrients;

3.6A — classify foods by the nutrients they provide;

Physical Education TEKS

K.10A — recognize that eating a variety of foods produces energy for physical activity;

K.10B — identify the best source of hydration during physical activity.

1.10A — identify healthy foods that produce energy for physical activity;

1.10B — identify different hydration options, including water, that enhance physical activity

2.10A — identify the types of food that produce energy to enhance physical activity;

2.10B — explain the need for proper hydration to enhance physical activity

3.10A — differentiate between healthy and unhealthy foods and their impact on sustainable energy for physical activity;

3.10B — differentiate between water and processed sugar or high-calorie drinks and their impact on sustainable energy for physical activity.

4.10A — examine the relationship between nutrition and optimal physical performance;

4.10B — explain the importance of proper hydration before, during, and after physical activity.

5.10A — identify healthy foods that enhance physical activity

5.10B — explain the importance of proper hydration before, during, and after physical activity

Science TEKS

3.5C — predict, observe, and record changes in the state of matter caused by heating or cooling such as ice becoming liquid water, condensation forming on the outside of a glass of ice water, or liquid water being heated to the point of becoming water vapor; and

3.5D — explore and recognize that a mixture is created when two materials are combined such as gravel and sand or metal and plastic paper clips

4.5A — measure, compare, and contrast physical properties of matter, including mass, volume, states (solid, liquid, gas), temperature, magnetism, and the ability to sink or float; and

4.5B — compare and contrast a variety of mixtures, including solutions.

5.5B — demonstrate that some mixtures maintain physical properties of their ingredients such as iron filings and sand and sand and water; and

5.5C — identify changes that can occur in the physical properties of the ingredients of solutions such as dissolving salt in water or adding lemon juice to water.

Common Core

CCSS.ELA-Literacy.W.K.8 — With guidance and support from adults, recall information from experiences or gather information from provided sources to answer a question

CCSS.ELA-Literacy.W.1.8 — With guidance and support from adults, recall information from experiences or gather information from provided sources to answer a question.

CCSS.ELA-Literacy.W.2.8 — Recall information from experiences or gather information from provided sources to answer a question.

CCSS.ELA-Literacy.W.3.8 — Recall information from experiences or gather information from print and digital sources; take brief notes on sources and sort evidence into provided categories.

CCSS.ELA-Literacy.W.4.8 — Recall relevant information from experiences or gather relevant information from print and digital sources; take notes, paraphrase, and categorize information, and provide a list of sources.

CCSS.ELA-Literacy.W.5.8 — Recall relevant information from experiences or gather relevant information from print and digital sources; summarize or paraphrase information in notes and finished work, and provide a list of sources.

ELL Accommodations

Sentence stems
Peer turn and talk
Think, pair, share
Extra time for responses
Rephrase, repeat, or slow down
Visuals and verbal cues to reinforce spoken and written language
Graphic organizers
Hands-on activities
Non-verbal responses

SPED Accommodations

Sentence stems
Choice regarding which herbs (and tea) to smell, touch, and taste
Use of computers and/or scribe for exploration guide
Shortened assignment
Additional time for completion
Breaks/PEAS area
Rephrase, repeat, or slow down
Drawing or model representation
Visuals and verbal cues
Visual schedule
Pre-teach vocabulary

© 2023 Partners for Education, Agriculture, and Sustainability

Fun and Easy PEASy Reflections

Building in reflection time at the end of lessons helps bring closure to an activity and give students the opportunity to connect newly learned concepts to their personal lives. Below are some reflection techniques that are easy to facilitate in a short amount of time and that you can revisit with a variety of outdoor lessons.

Word Whip

Have students circle up, or this can be done as they line up to transition to the next activity. Give them 15-30 seconds to think of a single word that sums up what they did or learned during the lesson. Get a volunteer or the line leader to start, and then quickly go around the class to share. If in line, this is best done outside so students can use their outside voices to ensure everyone can hear.

Rate this Lesson

Have students circle up, or this can be done as they line up to transition to the next activity. Ask them to rate the lesson using their fingers from a 1 (not good) to 5 (excellent). If in a group, have a few students with different ratings share why they rated the lesson the way they did. If time permits, allow all students to share.

Clear and Cloudy

Have students circle up. Go around the circle and have students share one thing they learned (what is clear) and one thing they are not sure about or would like to learn more about (what is still cloudy).

Rose, Bud, Thorn

Have students circle up. We will be taking three trips around this circle to allow everyone to share their Rose (highlight of the lesson), Bud (something they want to learn more about), and Thorn (a challenge they encountered). This activity is easy to facilitate and will take 15-30 minutes, so it may need to be an extension to the lesson itself.

Wonder Wall

A major goal for outdoor education is to stimulate curiosity and guide students in how they can find answers to their own questions. Create a space on a wall or bulletin board in your classroom and label it "Wonder Wall." At the end of your lesson, ask students to write down any questions that came up for them that did not get answered. These questions should be added to the Wonder Wall. When the teacher sees repeated or related questions, they should be grouped together for further exploration as a class. This wall can also become a springboard for research projects.

PART IV

Toolshed:
Resources

504 Plans and Accommodations
Creating a Welcoming Outdoor/Kitchen Class

For students with learning and physical differences who need adjustments to their learning environment to help them meet their needs in the classroom.

Advocacy
Why Outdoor Education

An activity by an individual or group that seeks to influence decisions within public institutions, such as education or governmental platforms.

Anchor chart
Engaging Lesson Rubric

A tool for learning. Like an anchor, it holds the concepts, objectives, and procedures for an outdoor educator's lesson in one place.

Antiracist Multicultural Practice
Why Outdoor Education

Teaching methods which seek to overcome systemic racism and all other forms of oppression.

Berms and Swales
Getting to Know Your Outdoor Learning Environment

Earthen barriers (berms) that act to concentrate rainwater in desired shallow depressions (swales) as it travels down a slope.

Binary (Human/Nature)
Introduction

Something having two parts and being characterized as separate.

BIPOC
Honor the Earth

An acronym for individuals who identify as Black, Indigenous, and People of Color.

Bloom's Taxonomy
Why Outdoor Education

A hierarchical ordering of cognitive abilities that can help teachers teach and students to learn.

CASEL
Overview of SEL/Ecotherapy

An acronym for Collaborative for Academic, Social, and Emotional Learning, a think tank founded in 1994 to provide high-quality evidence-based SEL (Social and Emotional Learning).

Culturally Responsive
Why Outdoor Education

A teaching practice that takes into account students' customs, characteristics, experiences, and perspectives as tools for rigorous and meaningful instruction.

Decolonizing Framework
Why Outdoor Education

Decolonizing framework is teaching with the intention to undo colonizing practices. Within an Outdoor Educational context, this means confronting and challenging the colonizing ideologies and policies that have influenced education and agriculture in the past, and which still exist today.

Decolonizing Pedagogical Practices
Overview of SEL/Ecotherapy

Decolonizing pedagogical practices are routines, methods, and speech which educators implement with the intention to undo colonizing practices. Within an Outdoor Educational context, this means confronting and challenging the colonizing ideologies and policies that have influenced education and agriculture in the past, and which still exist today.

Divergent Thinking
Why Outdoor Education

Creative thinking that may follow many lines of thought and tends to generate new and original solutions to problems.

Earth-Centered Education
Why Outdoor Education

An educational discipline not focused on living organisms but on the Earth as a whole. Educators uphold the belief that the Earth is for all and we must change our practices and mindset so that they align with the Earth's sustainability.

Ecological Awareness
Why Outdoor Education

A consciousness of the impact of our actions and activities on our environment and the ecosystems in our community. Pertains to awareness on an individual or collective, local, and global level.

Ecotherapy
Overview of SEL/Ecotherapy

Ecotherapy, also called nature therapy or green therapy, is the practice of spending time in outdoor spaces in order to improve physical and mental health.

Environmental Consciousness
Why Outdoor Education

When an individual is informed and aware of their effect upon the environment, and intentionally taking steps to ensure their impact is minimized.

Environmental Advocacy
Why Outdoor Education

Presenting information about the environment and environmental systems to others in an effort to encourage environmental protection or remediation.

Environmental Stewardship
Why Outdoor Education

The intentional care and protection of outdoor environments by means of responsible use and conservation which improve ecosystem sustainability.

Environmental Protection
Why Outdoor Education

The practice of implementing responsible and protecting systems of support for an outdoor environment such as maintaining the health of plants, animals, water, and air and soil quality.

Experiential Learning
Why Outdoor Education

The practice of learning by doing, especially hands-on activities.

Flexible Mindset
Why Outdoor Education

The synthesis of self-awareness, adaptive strategy use, and determination that supports students to grow and become independent learners.

Fossilized Thinking
Why Outdoor Education

Ways of thinking which are outdated, rigid, and never changing.

Functioning (Executive, Emotional, Survival State)
Background for Trauma-Informed Instruction)

A set of processes that are related to self-management in the brain which help regulate our ability to learn and achieve a goal (executive), process our emotions (emotional), and meet our basic needs (survival). When triggered by past traumas and experiences, some if not all of these systems can be altered, creating behavioral changes and challenges.

Holistic Approach
Overview of SEL/Ecotherapy

Relating to and taking into account whole systems and environments

Inclusion Setting
Outdoor Learning for All Abilities

A learning environment where students with learning differences are supported through individual learning goals, accommodations, and modifications so that they are able to access general education.

Interdependency
Why Outdoor Education

The dependence of two or more things upon each other, such as humans and our outdoor environments.

Kinesthetic Learning
Why Outdoor Education

Full-body movement to process new information, for example hand movements to memorize vocabulary or dance to remember lists of information. Kinesthetic learners comprehend best with items they can hold and hands-on examples.

Kinship
Why Outdoor Education

A sharing of characteristics or origins.

Leave No Trace
Top 10 Tips for Outdoor Lessons

The practice of leaving the land in the same (or better) condition as one finds it in.

Macrocosmic
Honor the Earth

When the universe is considered as a whole.

Metacognitive Practice
Setting Expectations

Methods and teaching skills to help students understand how they learn best.

Multisensory Learning
Why Outdoor Education

A discipline of teaching where students engage more than one sense (sight, hearing, touch, taste, smell) at a time to acquire knowledge through activation of different parts of the brain and different intelligences.

Multiple Intelligences Theory
Why Outdoor Education

A theory which explains different ways that students learn and obtain information, first created by Howard Gardner. Gardner proposes the existence of different forms of intelligence of which all people are on a spectrum, instead of one singular class of intelligence. The multiple intelligence theory speaks to eight different intelligences types: linguistic, spatial, logical/mathematical, kinesthetic, musical, interpersonal, intrapersonal, and naturalist.

Mushroom Blocks
Nature Nuggets

Mycelium (mushroom) spores within sawdust, grains, and other organic matter. Mushroom blocks are a great addition to soil enrichment, similar to compost.

Nature
Opportunities to Honor the Earth

They physical world together as a whole, including plants, animals, rocks, land, water, and all living and nonliving elements. Nature is everywhere and not a destination. We are part of nature.

Nature-Deficit Disorder
Why Outdoor Education

First labeled and identified by Richard Louvre. A condition where reduced experiences outdoors and in natural spaces negatively affect the educational development and emotional health of children (Louvre, 2015).

Naturalist and Spatial Intelligences
Why Outdoor Education

Two categories of intelligence as proposed originally by Howard Gardner (see Multiple Intelligences) which are utilized by the environmental, agricultural, and biological work forces, among other individuals who work in outdoor spaces. These intelligences are often neglected to be upheld and taught in traditional schooling.

Neo-Colonialism
Why Outdoor Education

The continued or re-imposed oppression by a historically colonial power.

Neurodivergent
Outdoor Learning for All Abilities

Brain organization/function that differs from the neurotypical.

Ollas
Nature Nuggets

A clay container with a narrow neck, ollas are a method of water irrigation which releases water into surrounding plants through a process called soil moisture tension. Ollas are buried in garden soil, reducing surface watering which promotes weeds.An outdoor place where a student can take a break to regulate emotions.

Open-Ended Questions
Creating a Welcoming Outdoor Classroom

A question that cannot be answered with a "yes" or "no," eliciting further elaboration, explanation, and critical thought.

Outdoor Learning Area
Introduction

A space for learning outdoors. Ideally includes a seating area, shade, water, and some natural elements.

PEAce Area
Creating a Welcoming Outdoor Kitchen/Classroom

An outdoor place where a student can take a break to regulate emotions.

Place-Based Outdoor Education
Why Outdoor Education

An educational philosophy which immerses students in the local community and environment to teach academic concepts and curriculum.

Restorative Practices
Why Outdoor Education

A teaching framework which resolves interpersonal issues in a cooperative and constructive way.

SEL
Overview of SEL/Ecotherapy

The natural and/or intentional process of developing self-awareness, self-control, interpersonal skills, and inner well-being.

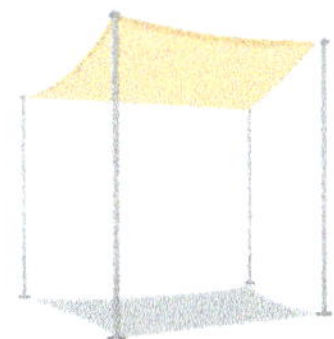

Shade Sails
Getting to Know Your Outdoor Learning Environment

A sun shade generally made of textiles that when mounted on posts creates a shaded area where students can gather.

Shinrin-yoku **(Forest Bathing)**
Overview of SEL/Ecotherapy)

The practice (originally developed by researchers in Japan) of systematically utilizing the positive health outcomes associated with time spent in nature.

Social Justice
Why Outdoor Education

The understanding that all individuals in a society should have full access to the same rights, privileges, and opportunities.

Stakeholder
What to Wear and Bring

A community member or other person with an interest or investment in your outdoor learning activities.

Symbiotic Relationships
Nature Nuggets

A mutually beneficial relationship between two or more living organisms.

Transplants
Nature Nuggets

Plants that were sprouted in pots or trays that can be moved to an outdoor garden.

Total Physical Response (TPR)

A method of teaching concepts by using physical movement to react to verbal input.

Trauma-Informed Instruction
Background for Trauma-Informed Instruction

An instructional model that emphasizes care, compassion, and acceptance of students who have experienced traumatic events, regardless of their successes or failures in an educational setting.

UV Index
Getting to Know Your Outdoor Learning Environment

The ultraviolet index is a standard of measurement that gauges the sun-burning potential of ultraviolet radiation for a given time and place.

Water Key
What to Wear and Bring

Allows you to gain access to an outside commercial water supply, such as those located outside many school buildings. Available for purchase from most hardware stores.

Waffle Garden
Getting to Know Your Outdoor Learning Environment

An indigenous farming system of sunken garden beds surrounded by dense clay-rich walls that often form a grid or waffle pattern.

© 2023 Partners for Education, Agriculture, and Sustainability

WORKS REFERENCED

From Why Outdoor Education?

Austin, S. (2022). The school garden in the primary school: Meeting the challenges and reaping the benefits. *Education 3-13*, 50(6), 707–721.

Avcı, G., Gümüş, N. (2020). The effect of Outdoor Education on the achievement and recall levels of primary school students in Social Studies courses. *Review of International Geographical Education*, 10(1), 171-206. Retrieved from http://www.rigeo.org/vol10no1/Number1Spring/RIGEO-V10-N1-9.pdf

Banks, J. A., & Banks, C.A. M. (2015). *Multicultural Education: Issues and perspectives (9th ed.).* Wiley Global Education US.

Depres, C. (2021, October 13). *Report: 1 in 5 latino youth have obesity.* Salud America. https://salud-america.org/report-1-in-5-latino-youth-have-obesity

Etherington, N. (2012). *Gardening for children with Autism Spectrum Disorders and Special Education needs: Engaging with nature to combat anxiety, promote sensory integration and build social Skills.* Jessica Kingsley Publishers.

Evans, A., Ranjit, N., Fair, C. N., Jennings, R., & Warren, J. L. (2016). Previous gardening experience and gardening enjoyment is related to vegetable preferences and consumption among low-income elementary school children. *Journal of Nutrition Education and Behavior*, 48(9), 618–624.

Fisher-Maltese, C. (2016). "We won't hurt you butterfly!" Second-graders become environmental stewards from experiences in a school garden. *The International Journal of Early Childhood Environmental Education*, 4(1), 54-69.

Fickman, Laurie. (2022). Study finds low Vitamin D levels in young people of color. University of Houston. Retrieved August 16, 2023 from https://www.uh.edu/news-events/stories/2022-news-articles/june-2022/06282022-vitamin-d-low-in-hispanic-black-adolescents-nursing-study.php

Lanza, K., Alcazar, M., Hoelscher, D. M., & Kohl, H. W. (2021). Effects of trees, gardens, and nature trails on heat index and child health: Design and methods of the Green Schoolyards Project. *BMC Public Health.* (21)98. https://doi.org/10.1186/s12889-020-10128-2

Lebrun-Harris, L.A., Ghandour, R.M., Kogan, M.D., & Warren, M.D. (2022). Five-year trends in US children's health and well-being, 2016-2020. *JAMA Pediatrics.* 176(7). doi:10.1001/jamapediatrics.2022.0056

Louv, R. (2005). *Last child in the woods: Saving our children from nature-deficit disorder.* Algonquin Books of Chapel Hill.

Lucas, A., Snider, A., & Shanhong Luo. (2018). Evaluating community support for an elementary school education garden. *Children, Youth and Environments,* 28(1), 42–65.

Rees-Punia, E., Holloway, A., Knauft, D., & Schmidt, M. D. (2017). Effects of school gardening lessons on elementary school children's physical activity and sedentary time. *Journal of Physical Activity and Health*, 14(12), 959–964.

Roberts, K., Wilcox, J., & Bahnson, A. (2021). Cultivating Place: Engaging students with Place-based learning in community gardens. *Science & Children*, 58(4), 53–60.

Romero, V., Foreman, J., Strang, C., Rodriguez, L., Payan, R., & Moore Bailey, K. (2019). Examining equitable and inclusive work environments in environmental education: Perspectives from the field and implications for organizations. *Lawrence Hall of Science.* http://beetlesproject.org/resources/equitable-and-inclusive-work-environments/

Schattenberg, P. (2021, March 2). *Initial Texas agricultural loss estimates from Uri exceed $600 million.* AgriLife Today. https://agrilifetoday.tamu.edu/2021/03/02/initial-ag-losses-from-uri-exceed-600-million/

Shiva, V. (2015). *Earth democracy: Justice, sustainability, and peace.* Society for the Study of Native Arts and Sciences, North Atlantic Books.

Sobel, D. (1999). *Beyond ecophobia: Reclaiming the heart in Nature Education.* Orion Society.

Swansea University. (2019, June 11). *An hour or two of outdoor learning every week increases teachers' job satisfaction.* ScienceDaily. Retrieved April 14, 2023 from www.sciencedaily.com/releases/2019/06/190611102710.htm

Tabari, M.A. & Tabari, I.A. (2015). Links between Bloom's Taxonomy and Gardner's Multiple Intelligences: The issue of textbook analysis. *Advances in Language and Literacy Studies.* 6(1), 94-101.

Waite, S., & Aronsson, J. (2022). Some impacts on health and well-being from school-based Outdoor Learning. In Jucker, R., & Au, J. van. (Ed. 1). *High-quality outdoor learning: Evidence-based education outside the classroom for children, teachers and society.* Springer.

From Setting Expectations and Guidelines for Fun and Safety

Gorski, P. (2017, November 26). *Beyond celebrating diversity: 20 things I will do to be an equitable educator.* The Equity Literacy Institute.http://www.edchange.org/handouts/20things.pdf

From Opportunities to Honor the Earth

Kimmerer, R.W. (2015). *Braiding sweetgrass: Indigenous wisdom, scientific knowledge and the teachings of plants.* Milkweed Editions.

From Background for Trauma-Informed Instruction

Bailey, B.A. (2015). *Conscious discipline.* ZCUOO Publishers.

From Holistic Benefits of Outdoor Learning

CASEL Framework. (n.d.). *What is the CASEL Framework? [Infographic].* Retrieved March 13, 2023 from https://casel.org/fundamentals-of-sel/what-is-the-casel-framework/#interactive-casel-wheel.

Fitzgerald, S. (2019, October 19). *The secret to mindful travel? A walk in the woods.* National Geographic. https://www.nationalgeographic.com/travel/article/forest-bathing-nature-walk-health

Laguaite, M. (2021, April 13). *Do you need a nature prescription?.* WebMD. https://www.webmd.com/balance/features/ nature-therapy-ecotherapy.

Frontiers. (2019, April 4). *Stressed? Take a 20-minute "nature pill": Just 20 minutes of contact with nature will lower stress hormone levels, reveals new study.* ScienceDaily. Retrieved Mar 17, 2023 from www.sciencedaily.com/releases/2019/04/190404074915.html

Miyazaki, Y. (2021). *Shinrin-yoku: the Japanese way of forest bathing for health & relaxation.* Aster.

CURRICULUM AND PROFESSIONAL DEVELOPMENT RESOURCES

4H
Kids and teens complete hands-on projects in areas like science, health, agriculture, and civic engagement, in a positive environment where they receive guidance from adult mentors and are encouraged to take on proactive leadership roles.

www.4-h.org/programs

AmeriCorps
Members and volunteers serve directly with nonprofit organizations to tackle pressing challenges. They work to make service to others an indispensable part of the American experience.

www.americorps.gov/about/what-we-do

Bee Cause
Seeks to inspire the next generation of environmental stewards while protecting our planet's precious pollinators. With the support of their partners, they provide grants to help schools and organizations install and maintain their own observation hives.

www.thebeecause.org/resources

Big Green
Helping people grow their own food—with garden-based education, scalable, modular garden products and systems, and a community of support and collaboration.

www.biggreen.org/resources

City Blossoms
Since 2008, City Blossoms has designed, developed, collaborated on, and provided programming or trainings for over 100 projects throughout Washington, DC and nationwide.

www.cityblossoms.org/resources

Children and Nature Network
Supports and mobilizes leaders, educators, activists, practitioners, and parents working to turn the trend of an indoor childhood back out to the benefits of nature—and to increase safe and equitable access to the natural world for all.

www.childrenandnature.org/resource-hub/resources/

FoodCorps
AmeriCorps members serve alongside educators and school nutrition leaders to provide kids with nourishing meals, food education, and culturally affirming experiences with food that celebrate and nurture the whole child.

www.foodcorps.org/skillet/?p-type=resources

Green Schoolyards America
Inspires and supports systems change to transform asphalt-covered school grounds into living schoolyards that improve children's well-being, learning, and play, while strengthening their communities' ecological health and climate resilience.

www.greenschoolyards.org

Junior Master Gardener
An international youth gardening program of the university cooperative Extension network. JMG engages children in novel, "hands-on" group and individual learning experiences that provide a love of gardening, develop an appreciation for the environment, and cultivate the mind.

www.jmgkids.us/

KidGardening.Org
Supports educators and caregivers who bring the life-changing benefits of gardening to kids.

www.kidsgardening.org

LifeLab
Cultivates children's love of learning, healthy food, and nature through garden-based education.

www.lifelab.org

Native Land Digital
A not-for-profit organization, incorporated in December 2018. Native Land Digital is Indigenous-led, with an Indigenous Executive Director and majority Indigenous Board of Directors who oversee and direct the complex issues that mapping Indigenous territories involves.

www.native-land.ca/

PALS
The Peer Assistance and Leadership program enables young people to use their potential to make a difference in their lives, schools, and communities.

www.palusa.org

PEAS
A non-profit with the mission to cultivate joyful connections with the natural world through outdoor learning and edible education.

www.peascommunity.org

SGSO
The School Garden Support Organization is an open peer-to-peer learning network with the goal of growing, sustaining, and elevating a movement of equitable garden-based education.

www.sgsonetwork.org

© 2023 Partners for Education, Agriculture, and Sustainability

Slow Food USA
Aims to reconnect youth with their food by teaching them how to grow, cook, and enjoy real food.

https://slowfoodusa.org/school-gardens/

Texas A&M Agrilife Extension Offices
Provide training, publications, apps, and programs to bring Texans the latest research in agriculture, natural resources, and life sciences.

www.agrilifeextension.tamu.edu/

Texas Junior Master Naturalists
Provide youth ages 9-13 with an understanding of Texas' plants, water, soils, and wildlife while volunteering in local communities and developing a sense of stewardship in our environment.

www.txmn.org/resources/jrmastnat/

Whole Kids Foundation
Dedicated to helping kids eat better—and enjoy it! This nonprofit 501(c)(3) founded by Whole Foods Market is guided by the same values, principles, expertise, and standards for quality ingredients, food production methods, and nutrition.

www.wholekidsfoundation.org/school-gardens

CULTURALLY RELEVANT READ-ALOUD RESOURCE SAMPLER

This list was curated by Neha Shah, district and school garden leader, for a joint presentation we lead together.

City Green
by DyAnne DiSalvo-Ryan

Community Soup
by Alma Fullerton

Farmer Will Allen and the Growing Table
by Jacqueline Briggs Martin

Fry Bread: A Native American Family Story
by Kevin Noble Maillard

Gardening with Children
(Brooklyn Botanic Garden Guides for a Greener Planet)

Gathering the Sun: An Alphabet in Spanish and English
by Alma Flor Ada

Growing Vegetable Soup
by Lois Ehlert

How a Seed Grows
by Helene J. Jordan

In the Garden with Dr. Carver
by Susan Grigsby

Kids' Garden: 50 Hands-on Activities for All Seasons
by Whitney Cohen

My First Garden
by Wendy Cheyette Lewison

Our Community Garden
by Barbara Pollak

Our School Garden!
by Rick Swann

Plant a Little Seed
by Bonnie Christensen

Rainbow Stew
by Cathryn Falwell

Rice Is Life
by Rita Golden Gelman

Seedfolks
by Paul Fleischman

The Barefoot Book of Earth Tales
by Dawn Casey and Anne Wilson

The Good Garden: How One Family Went from Hunger to Having Enough
by Katie Smith Milway

The Jumbo Book of Gardening
by Karyn Morris

The Ugly Vegetables
by Grace Lin

What's in the Garden?
by Marianne Berkes

© 2023 Partners for Education, Agriculture, and Sustainability

OUTDOOR FREE-TIME CHOICE LIST

Go Earthing

Walk barefoot to feel the earth
with your feet in a designated space.

Plant a seed in a pot

Sit with a friend near your favorite plant and talk

Pull weeds

It is best to reflect and inform ourselves
on whether a plant is truly a non-beneficial
weed before uprooting them.

Take the temperature of the soil

Water the plants

Pour low and slow, to the roots of the plant.

Walk around with the Outdoor educator and talk about the garden

Collect seeds

Sort seeds

Expired seeds can also be used for crafts!

Make a Pattern or Design

(using approved plants or seeds)

Write a poem

Draw a picture

Do yoga

Use your body to grow from a seed into a plant!

Come up with your own idea!

ACKNOWLEDGEMENTS

This guidebook would never have come to fruition without the help, encouragement, and guidance from a host of impressive people in the Outdoor Education movement.

We would like to give a super special thank-you to our co-author Lauren Reneé Salinas-Garcia for bringing us along on her journey of connecting with her Indigenous roots. In sharing her worldview with us, she ensures that we always keep in the front of our minds that we **ARE** nature. It is essential for our lives and our planet that this message is shared with our community.

We would like to thank the following people for reviewing this guidebook in its entirety and giving us immensely valuable feedback: Maria Alverdi, Mariana Bonilla, Tiona Bell, Neha Shah, Kate Martin, Madison Phillips, and Jackie Vay.

We would like to give additional shout-outs to Mariana Bonilla for contributing the Shapes in Nature lesson, to Maria Alverdi for piloting the Shapes in Nature lesson with her students, to Kate Martin for adding to and refining PEAS Top Ten Tips to make them as clear and impactful as they are today, to Juiliet Whitsett for inclusion of her inspiring and beautiful artwork to our lessons, and to Neha Shah for curating the Culturally Relevant Read-Aloud Sampler.

We would also like to thank our editor, Kate Rowe, for her patience, thoroughness, and encouragement as we worked through the process together, and graphic designer, Callie Gabbert sharing her vast knowledge and immense talents with us through her illustrations and layout out of the book.

Lastly, this guidebook would not have been possible without the financial support and backing of the Sprouts Healthy Communities Foundation. We are truly grateful for their encouragement to continue this project beyond the impacts of the pandemic. Sprouts funding allowed PEAS to allocate our teams' members with precious time to bring this guidebook to life.

Thank you from all of us!

www.ingramcontent.com/pod-product-compliance
Lightning Source LLC
Chambersburg PA
CBHW040210110726
48005CB00019B/2963